j.s.bach

compact companions

PHILIPS *Classics*

COMPACT COMPANIONS

J. S. BACH

CHRISTOPHER HEADINGTON

SIMON & SCHUSTER

NEW YORK LONDON TORONTO SYDNEY TOKYO SINGAPORE

SIMON & SCHUSTER
ROCKEFELLER CENTER
1230 AVENUE OF THE AMERICAS
NEW YORK, NEW YORK 10020

Designed by Wherefore Art? Edited by Emma Lawson

Printed in Singapore by Imago Publishing Ltd
10 9 8 7 6 5 4 3 2 1

Library of Congress Cataloging-in-Publication Data
Headington, Christopher
Bach : a listener's guide to the classics / by Christopher Headington.
p. cm. — (Compact companions)
Discography: p.
ISBN 0-671-88788-2
1. Bach, Johann Sebastian, 1685–1750. 2. Composers—Germany—Biography. I. Title. II. Series.
ML410.B1H345 1994
780'.92—dc20
[B]   93-39718
CIP
MN

CONTENTS

Inside the present-day Bachhaus (Bach Museum) at Eisenach

Childhood and Schooldays

A sk anyone to name three of the greatest classical composers, and the chances are that Johann Sebastian Bach will be among them. Along with Beethoven and Mozart, he is almost a household name and his music has even been featured as the theme for a TV commercial in Britain, the 'Air on the G string', from his Third Orchestral Suite happily accompanying the scene of a man contentedly smoking a Hamlet cigar – whose brand name reminds us of another cultural giant, Shakespeare.

Was Bach the Shakespeare of music? Not really, for against the Englishman's wide-ranging plots, characteristic of an imaginative inheritor of Renaissance ideas, Bach's is a far more closely focused world centering on his own time and the north-German society in which he lived, with its princes, prelates and poverty. Indeed, his music reflects his whole career as a working musician in courts and churches. Unlike his great German contemporary Handel, born in the same year, Bach composed no operas, although his treatment of the Passion story in his *St. Matthew Passion* is as dramatic as anyone could wish, and while Handel became a wealthy impresario and remained a bachelor, Bach was never his own master and took on heavy family responsibilities. Thus, although he must have written his six Brandenburg Concertos partly for his own pleasure, they were also composed for the court orchestras of his employers Duke Wilhelm of Weimar and Prince Leopold of Anhalt-Cöthen, and then dedicated to yet another nobleman in whose court they were apparently not played at all. Similarly, his composition of over three hundred church cantatas may have been enjoyable work, but writing them was also his duty as an organist and choirmaster in several Lutheran churches, culminating in his final and longest-lasting appointment as a Kantor at Leipzig who provided and directed

Bach's father,
Johann Ambrosius Bach.
aged forty,
in the year of his
illustrious son's birth

the music of the city's principal churches.

His background was both ordinary and extraordinary. Ordinary, because his family was far from wealthy, and extraordinary because its profession was music. Even before he was born, on March 21, 1685, his was the greatest family of German musicians of the eighteenth century. The *New Grove Dictionary of Music and Musicians* lists around eighty Bachs, beginning with men such as Hans Bach (c.1555–1615), a violinist and entertainer at the ducal court of Württemberg. There is a picture of him with a fiddle in one hand and what may be a roll of music in the other (it could be a drinking cup), and it was said of him, 'When you hear him you have to laugh'.

Engraving of Eisenach, with Wartburg mountain in background, by Friedrich Rossmäsler (1775–1858)

The house at Eisenach where Bach was born. It no longer stands

Sebastian's father, Johann Ambrosius Bach, was a church organist and violinist in the town of Eisenach in Thuringia, around a hundred miles to the west (and slightly south) of Leipzig. A respected 'municipal musician' who belonged to a players' guild, he played twice a day at the town hall and also acted as an assistant to his cousin Johann Christoph Bach, the organist of St. George's Church. Sebastian's mother Maria was the daughter of a furrier.

This sounds a secure background. Yet Sebastian was born in an age when health and longevity were not to be taken for granted. He was one of eight children, but only four of them survived into adulthood, and his mother died in May 1694. His father remarried later in the year, for he could hardly bring up his children alone, but then he too died, in February 1695. His widow applied to the Eisenach town council for help, but little came her way and the family was broken up. Thus, by the age of nine Sebastian had lost his parents and also his home.

However, his father had given him his first instruction in music, both in keyboard and violin playing, and after three years' attendance at a good grammar school, the Lateinschule, he was already showing promise and strength of character. After he had lost both parents, his oldest brother Johann Christoph, already a professional musician at twenty-four and the principal organist of the nearby town of Ohrdruf, took him in and became his musical mentor. It was now that his special talent became increasingly evident on the keyboard instruments of the time, namely the organ, harpsichord and clavichord. His brother found him an apt pupil, and also began teaching him the basic

A panorama of Lüneburg, in a copperplate engraving

skills of composition. The boy sang, too, as a chorister in his brother's church and so earned a small salary, which helped pay for his keep. The only problem may have been his sheer precocity. He became interested in a set of new keyboard compositions in his brother's library, but Johann Christoph thought them too advanced for him and locked them away. According to some accounts, he then started getting up at night to pry them through the latticed front of the locked bookcase and copy them secretly, but was discovered by his brother and had his manuscript confiscated, only getting it back later, perhaps when he left his brother's home.

Sebastian stayed in Ohrdruf for five years, attending the Lyceum, a strict but well-regarded school, where he studied, among other things, Lutheran orthodoxy, Latin, history and mathematics and seemingly excelled among his fellows. It has been claimed that he was always a year or more younger than his classmates, but this may be a pious exaggeration. However, on March 15, 1700, six days before his fifteenth birthday, he left his brother's home and moved to a new school in Lüneburg, a town not far from Hamburg and some two hundred miles to the north of Ohrdruf. There were probably several reasons for the move: Johann Christoph now had two children of his own and his wife was expecting a third, so that living, as he did, in a smallish cottage, he could hardly continue to accommodate his teenage brother. At the same time Sebastian was probably ready to seek wider horizons, and seems to have been influenced by one of his schoolmasters at the Lyceum, Elias Herda, who had himself been educated at the Lüneburg school, St. Michael's.

The school was linked to a church, the Michaeliskirche, and was for commoners, including poorer boys with good voices such as Bach himself. With an older schoolfriend from Ohrdruf who probably accompanied him on his journey, Sebastian joined one of the two church choirs, the *Mettenchor* or Matins choir. In return, he was given free schooling, board and lodging and a share of fees earned at weddings and other such occasions. Although his treble voice may have broken fairly soon after his arrival, he continued to sing and became a 'choir prefect'.

At the same time, he continued his general studies and among his subjects were religious instruction (Lutheranism), Latin, mathematics, history and geography, German poetry and the physical sciences. But music remained his chief interest and skill, and he developed what was to become a lifelong interest in organs and organ building. He must have been pleased to find that the church's extensive music library, founded in 1555, contained words by other members of the Bach family, including his Eisenach uncle, Johann Christoph Bach. Still more importantly, its thousand volumes represented the work of nearly two hundred composers. Some of them were of the German

Heinrich Schütz in 1660

school, ranging from Heinrich Schütz (1585–1672) to Dietrich Buxtehude (1637–1707), Danish-born but now one of Germany's most celebrated organists. But there was also music of other countries with correspondingly different styles. Although we do not know what access Sebastian had to this material, he may have seen and studied works by such major musicians as the Netherlander Orlande de Lassus

(1532–94), a master of vocal polyphony, and Claudio Monteverdi (1567–1643), the great Italian composer of operas and madrigals.

It was also at this time that Sebastian got to know and appreciate the music of Georg Böhm, the organist at another Lüneburg church. This energetic musician and skillful composer much admired the organist Johann Adam Reincken, who occupied a church post in Hamburg and was now nearly eighty. Prompted by Böhm and perhaps accompanied by him, Sebastian more than once made the journey to Hamburg to hear Reincken play, necessarily traveling on foot and taking a day or more to cover the thirty miles or so. Once there, he may have stayed with his cousin, Johann Ernst Bach.

Orlande de Lassus by Hans Mielich, dating from 1571

On one such occasion, he sat enraptured as the aged Reincken improvised at the excellent Catharinenkirche organ on the hymn melody 'By the Waters of Babylon.' He also probably heard some performances at the Hamburg opera house, which was later to attract the talents of the young Handel. According to a story that his children told in later years, he was once returning alone from Hamburg to Lüneburg and, exhausted, sat down outside an inn, wishing that he had the money to go in and eat. Suddenly, someone threw out two herrings'

The great
Italian composer,
Claudio Monteverdi,
in 1640

A copperplate engraving of Zell (Celle), 1650, by Matthäus Merian

heads which fell in front of him. On picking them up he found a gift of Danish coins inside, which allowed him to satisfy his hunger and thirst and left enough over for another visit to Hamburg.

Thus, these teenage years in Lüneburg were of immense value to the gifted youth with his willingness and ability to learn all he could from differing musical sources. Another inspiration came through the Ritteracademie, a companion school to St. Michael's, where wealthier boys learned such social arts as fencing, dancing and speaking French. The dancing master there was Thomas de la Selle, a Frenchman and a former pupil of the French composer Lully. He was also a violinist in a largely French orchestra at the ducal court of Celle, some fifty miles away, to which a French-born duchess had brought much of her native culture. After befriending Sebastian, de la

Undated portrait,
by an unknown artist,
of the great
French composer
François Couperin

Selle took him there several times to hear French dance music in the duke's small private theater, and he may even have joined in as a violinist. In the chapel, he heard French organ music played by a French musician, Louis Gaudon, and elsewhere at court he heard and liked the harpsichord music of François Couperin (1668–1733), then still a young man but later to be a major figure in French music, enjoying a little rondeau by him enough to make a personal copy and noting down some of the grace notes and ornaments that made French keyboard music lighter and more decorative than German.

At around the time of his seventeenth birthday in 1702, Sebastian left Lüneburg and returned to his native Thuringia. The two years at St. Michael's, together with his other musical experiences, had fitted him for the professional musical career which lay before him, and he now sought employment as a church organist. Doubtless, he hoped that he, too, might become a Böhm, a Buxtehude or a Reincken; he may even have sensed that he possessed gifts which could take him still further.

Within the next few months, two posts became vacant. One was at the church of St. Jacobi in Sangerhausen, and in the summer of 1702 Sebastian applied for it. He was interviewed and auditioned, and then accepted the post, but the reigning duke intervened in favor of an older and more experienced candidate of his own choice. The other was the position of organist at St. George's Church in Eisenach, held, until his death early in 1703, by Johann Christoph Bach. However, it seems unlikely that, as an eighteen-year-old, Sebastian would have applied; at any rate, it went to yet another Bach, his cousin Johann Bernhard, nine years his senior.

For a while, therefore, Sebastian marked time, and we know that in March 1703 he was working as a violinist at the court of Duke Johann Ernst of Weimar and playing in a chamber orchestra. It seems that he also sometimes played the organ in the ducal chapel, since the court organist Johann Effler, a friend of the Bach family, was elderly and in fragile health. Sebastian must have been well thought of, since he also taught music to the duke's sons, the younger of whom learned to compose. At this time, too, he benefited from getting to know the celebrated Weimar violinist Johann Paul von Westhoff, a pioneer in the technique of double-stopping and the first musician to compose unaccompanied works for the instrument. However, his sights remained set on obtaining a church post and finally, in August 1703, he became the organist of the Neukirche at Arnstadt, a town some thirty-five miles south east of Eisenach. He was now eighteen, and his childhood and formal musical apprenticeship were over.

Arnstadt

The Arnstadt appointment came about following the installation of a new organ. The instrument was ready by June 1703 and although an organist, Andreas Börner, was already nominally in place, the church authorities called on Bach to inaugurate it on July 13 and paid him a fee for doing so. Perhaps they already had it in mind to offer this exceptionally gifted young man the post of organist over Börner's head. At any rate, to avoid ill-feeling they assigned Börner to other work and asked Bach to accept the position. A month later he received his formal contract with the seal of the reigning Count Anton Günther.

This document tells us much about the social structure and manners of the time. It stated that Bach should 'cultivate the fear of God, sobriety and the love of peace, altogether avoiding bad company and any distraction from your calling, and generally conducting yourself in all things towards God, high authority and your superiors as befitting an honor-loving servant and organist'. In particular, he was enjoined to be 'faithful, gracious and obedient to his High County Grace'. In return for all this, and performing his musical duties with skill and diligence, he was to be paid an annual salary of fifty guilders and an allowance for board and lodging. This was higher than usual for a first post, and more than some of his relatives received even as experienced musicians. He was able to buy himself a harpsichord and acquire the first books of what was to become a respectable library. During his first year he seems to have lodged in one of the Arnstadt inns, the Golden Crown. This was also the residence of his second cousin, Maria Barbara Bach, and they soon became friends.

Bach's duties were reasonably light, involving two hours in church for the Sunday morning service, playing for further services on Mondays and Thursdays, and providing music for a prayer hour on Tuesdays. In general, he simply accompanied the hymns sung by the congregation and a choir, which he himself recruited, all male and consisting of boys and students. Thus he had ample free time, but we know little of how he spent it. He may have participated in the town's other musical activities, since these included court and theater music. He may even have helped with the composition of a *Singspiel* (musical play) about beer-brewing which took place in May 1705, perhaps with some of his choir taking part, for the local tax on beer helped to pay his salary. Its music, however, has been lost.

Indeed, up to this time there is little evidence of his work as a composer. It is certain that many student works have been lost, and it would be interesting to see them, for not even a genius such as Bach can become a master composer without learning his craft through supervised exercises and private experiments. However, from now on compositions survive with names and dates. (In 1950, 200 years after Bach's death, all

Arnstadt, in a copperplate engraving by Matthäus Merian

of his known compositions were catalogued by the musicologist Wolfgang Schmieder. His *Bach Werke-Verzeichnis* (BWV) is now accepted as the standard means of numbering the composer's works.) One is his *Capriccio on the Departure of a Beloved Brother* BWV992, a harpsichord piece probably written in 1703, when his brother Jakob, three years older than he, went to join a military band in Sweden. Unlike church music of the time, it is programatic in content in a way that we associate more with later, Romantic composers. Thus, drooping chromatic phrases in the right hand, in the somber key of F minor, are supposed to depict the sorrow of friends and relatives as Jakob takes his leave. The four movements, of which three are slow, are labeled with their meaning: the first portrays people trying to dissuade Jakob from his journey, the second shows their fears of what may befall him, the third is a lament, and the busy finale is the leavetaking itself, which includes the sounds of the departing stagecoach and a vigorous 'postilion's fugue'. In fact, Jakob traveled as far as Constantinople (now Istanbul), before dying in Stockholm in 1722 at the age of forty. He and Sebastian never met again. This colorful Capriccio shows that Bach could imbue his music with a keen sense of mood. Although in later life he rarely used such a revealing title, his most characteristic music is expressive rather than abstract, and when he actually chose to tell a story, as in his great *St. Matthew Passion*, the result is highly dramatic. In other words, he was not only a master of his craft, but also a man of flesh and blood, as an incident in the summer of 1705 showed. A student named Johann Geyersbach, an unskilled bassoonist who played at the Neukirche, and was actually older than Bach himself, was rudely told by the young organist that he sounded like a goat. Not surprisingly, he took offense and on August 4, 1705, returning from a christening and doubtless slightly drunk, he took his revenge. On meeting Bach and Maria Barbara's elder sister in the street, he demanded an apology. Bach refused, and Geyersbach struck him with his stick, calling him a *Hundsfott*, or cur. Bach then drew a knife, but the others present separated the two. Bach complained to his church authorities, saying that he could not safely go about if Geyersbach were not punished and restrained, but they told him that he was himself partly responsible for the affray. Both young men were admonished.

Bach was already unhappy in Arnstadt and this incident did nothing to help matters. The church council had soon discovered that their brilliant young organist was also a touchy youth who had a mind of his own and was not afraid to express it forcefully. In October 1705, soon after the Geyersbach affair, he asked his cousin Johann Ernst Bach to deputize for him at the Neukirche and obtained a month's leave so that he could travel to Lübeck and hear Buxtehude play the magnificent organ at the Marienkirche. This was a journey of nearly three hundred miles, which he is said to have made partly on foot. The great Danish organist, then nearly seventy and approaching retirement, also directed concerts in the weeks leading up to Christmas, which Bach evidently attended. He may also have been present at a grand concert in memory of the Emperor Leopold I, who had died earlier in the year. It is just possible that he hoped to succeed Buxtehude in his post. However, a condition for this which would have deterred him was that the next organist should marry Buxtehude's daughter. She was ten years older than he and no beauty, and he may also by now have been contemplating marriage with Maria Barbara.

He remained in Lübeck until about the beginning of February 1706, having much overstayed his leave, and on returning to Arnstadt he had to make his excuses to the irate church authorities, who summoned him to Count Anton's palace on February 21 and demanded an explanation. They were even angrier when he defiantly justified his absence by saying he had been improving his musical skills in their interests and reproached him on other grounds, saying that he had failed to maintain good relations with his choir and should perform more concerted music with them, in other words the kind of church cantatas of which he later produced so many. He replied that he could play the organ for such occasions, but only if the church council provided a conductor. Yet another complaint was that he upset and confused churchgoers by making 'surprising variations' when playing hymns, indulging himself in improvisatory freedom instead of playing the plain accompaniments that his provincial congregation expected. Bach agreed to desist, and then deliberately stripped his playing down to an unmusical minimum. The church council knew that he was making fools of them, but could do little about it since he could claim that he was acting precisely as ordered. As a result, his relations with his employers were permanently soured.

This story says much about the young Bach. His musical ability could be heard and appreciated by all, but he was not a good subordinate and his sturdy independence of mind already marked him out before he was twenty. One of his modern biographers, Malcolm Boyd, writes of him at this time: 'As someone scarcely out of his teens, he must have appeared intolerably arrogant and self-willed, and, whatever posterity may think, the consistory had every right to question whether what Bach did for the Neukirche merited the salary they paid him.' Harsh, but probably fair, comment.

Later in 1706 he was once again in trouble with his employers for his poor control of his choristers, who sometimes played ball during church services, carried knives into school and frequented establishments of ill repute. As someone of much the same age as these youths, he had little chance of controling them, but he was still held responsible. The church council also took him to task for inviting a 'stranger maiden' to his organ loft, but here he was able to show that he had obtained permission and that she had been singing to his accompaniment. She was almost certainly his future wife, Maria Barbara. The writing was on the wall, however, and he must have known that it was time for him to leave Arnstadt and seek a more congenial position. Even without his disagreements with his employers, it was clear that he had little hope of doing anything musically interesting or ambitious in Arnstadt.

His chance of a move came in December 1706 with the death of Johann Georg Ahle, the organist of St. Blasius' Church, Mühlhausen. Lying some twenty miles north east of Eisenach, this imperial free city was governed by an elected council rather than a nobleman, and the church of St. Blasius, one of its two principal churches, was an imposing building with a strong musical tradition. Its council already had in mind a successor to Ahle, but at the suggestion of a council member related to Bach by marriage, the young Johann Sebastian was invited to attend for a *Probe*, or audition, on April 24, 1707. On June 14, he was interviewed again and told the church council that he wished to receive the same salary as at Arnstadt. Although this was more that

Emperor Leopold I in armor,
painted in 1658 by Guido Cagnacci

Ahle had earned, the council agreed and offered him the post. They also provided a wagon to move his belongings. Later that month, he resigned from his Arnstadt post, where he was succeeded by Johann Ernst Bach.

Bach was now twenty-two, and we can take further stock of the music that he had by now composed. His Cantata No. 4, *Christ lag in Todes banden*, may have been written for his *Probe* at Mühlhausen: based on a Lutheran chorale (hymn) melody as so many of his cantatas are, it is scored for solo voices and choir plus cornett, trombones, strings and a keyboard continuo (accompaniment) played on the organ. But because some of his early pieces were exercises based on the music of other composers, remain unsigned and undated, or exist only in the form of copies made by others, uncertainties remain. One book on the composer describes his Pastorale in F major, BWV590, as among the best pieces of the Arnstadt years and an 'exquisite gem of sustained lyricism,' but immediately adds that its authenticity is 'under suspicion'. On the other hand, *Grove* lists it as authentic, but assigns it to around 1710. Some scholars believe they have identified some twenty works of the Arnstadt period, but others are more cautious. Among the earliest ones that are certainly by Bach are the 'departure' Capriccio for his brother Jakob, the one-movement harpsichord Capriccio in E major, probably written in 1704, which is inscribed 'in honor of' his Ohrdruf brother Johann Christoph, and a lively keyboard Sonata in D, BWV963, with a theme imitating hens and roosters. Three harpsichord Toccatas, BWV913–915, alternate brilliant passagework and more stately music: as regards their date, *Grove* merely says 'before 1708'. Even so, they are evidence of the future great composer experimenting. Bach's nineteenth-century biographer Philipp Spitta thought the E minor Toccata, the second of these, 'one of those pieces steeped in melancholy which Bach alone could write', and it is worth noticing that all three are in minor keys. However, it has been suggested that the final

The organ of the Neukirche at Arnstadt, completed in 1703, photographed in 1910

section of this piece is a reworking of an existing Italian one.

This is another reminder that Bach studied all the music that came his way and caught his interest, whether it were German, French or Italian. In later life, he was not ashamed to admit how much he had learned from the music of others. After his death, his son Carl Philipp Emanuel wrote of his father's early studies of organ music by Reincken, Buxtehude, the German organist Nicolaus Bruhns and the French one Nicolas de Grigny, information which he must have been given by Johann Sebastian himself.

But for all Bach's wide-ranging interest in other musical schools and styles, his roots were still in the music of the Lutheran church services, in whose traditions he had been raised. In his early twenties he also composed organ pieces based on chorale melodies, such as his treatment of the hymn tunes, *Wie schön leuchtet der Morgenstern*, BWV739, of which we have a manuscript copy probably in his own hand, the earliest one known to exist. There is also the Chorale Prelude *Gelobet seist du, Jesu Christ*, BWV722, which intersperses simple statements of each phrase of the tune with rich, improvisatory flourishes. Although we do not know whether this was written at Arnstadt or in Mühlhausen, it is likely that it was the elaborate kind of music, the 'sundry embellishments' that, according to his Arnstadt employers, simply confused a congregation.

By now, Bach had also composed brilliant, original pieces for the organ which showed off his finger dexterity and no less remarkable command of the pedal keyboard operated by the feet. These preludes and fugues include those listed as BWV531 and 533 and also BWV550 and 551. There are also fantasias, more free-ranging in shape as the name suggests, such as BWV563, 570 and 572.

But by far the best known piece belonging to these years is the Toccata and Fugue in

Dietrich Buxtehude, in Johannes Voorhout's painting (1674) depicting the friendship between himself and fellow organist Reincken

D minor, BWV565. This is immensely dramatic music which raises splendid cathedrals of sound and seems to revel in mystery and mastery; timeless in its appeal, this music, arranged for a modern symphony orchestra, even inspired a memorable sequence in Walt Disney's 1940 film *Fantasia*. Probably written at around the time of Bach's twenty-first birthday in 1706, it shows, unmistakably, that this awkward young man had already earned his place in musical history. Of course he had inherited and profited from existing traditions of organ music, but this brilliant yet dignified Toccata and Fugue demonstrated that he was to enrich them still further.

Mühlhausen

Bach arrived in Mühlhausen in the first few days of July 1707 and at once established himself as a composer as well as an organist. It may have been in this month that he composed his Cantata, *Aus der Tiefen rufe ich, Herr, zu dir*, a penitential work whose title is the biblical 'Out of the depths I cry unto thee, O Lord'. (Its number in the standard listing of Bach's cantatas is 131, but this bears no relation to its date of composition, and the same is true of Cantata No. 106, mentioned below.) The somber mood of this music for voices and orchestra, written for another Mühlhausen church (that of St. Mary) and for a commemorative service following a serious fire in the city, hardly reflected his own probably hopeful state of mind but reminds us that, like any other church composer of his time, he was supposed to express pious community sentiments rather than exhibit his own soul. Similarly, when serving as a court musician, he wrote to satisfy his noble employer. As far as we know, he accepted this state of affairs throughout his life without complaint.

A month after he reached Mühlhausen, his maternal great-uncle Tobias Lämmerhirt died. He probably wrote his Cantata No. 106 for the funeral, which took place on August 14; its title is *Gottes Zeit ist die allerbeste Zeit* ('God's Time is the Best'), although it is now sometimes also called the *Actus tragicus*. Here is music which powerfully sets the Old Testament message of mortality against the Christian reassurance of salvation, and sums all up with trust in God. Somber though thoughts of death might be, Bach himself was surely a happy man, for his relative left him fifty guilders, more than half his annual salary of eighty-five guilders. This undoubtedly helped him to enter into his marriage to his second cousin Maria Barbara Bach. The wedding took place on

October 17, at the village church in Dornheim, near Arnstadt, whose pastor Johann Lorenz Stauber was a friend of them both (a year later he married Maria Barbara's aunt). Six months older than Sebastian, Maria Barbara was also a musician, and two sons born to the young couple, Wilhelm Friedemann in 1710 and Carl Philipp Emanuel in 1714, were themselves to gain fame in their father's profession.

Bach's future now looked secure. But once again, and soon, he found himself less than happy in his job. Although his dealings with his Mühlhausen church council were amicable, he realized that his opportunities for writing concerted music for the Blasiuskirche were limited, for its pastor, Johann Adolf Frohne, inclined towards the German Pietist movement which resembled English Puritanism, liked church music to be simple. In practice, this meant that he wanted it mainly restricted to the plain singing of hymns and liturgical texts. Bach quickly became frustrated, and his temperament did not take kindly to the situation. Furthermore, Pastor Frohne was on poor personal terms with the pastor of the Marienkirche, Georg Christian Eilmar, for whom Bach had composed Cantata No. 131, and who believed that elaborate music had its role in church services.

Indeed, the founder of Lutheranism, Martin Luther, had himself been a musician, and had stated, 'Music is a beautiful and lovely gift of God and a queen over every movement of the human heart; nothing on earth is more powerful than noble music'. This was certainly also Bach's belief, but Pastor Frohne seems to have considered that anything beyond the simplest church music smacked of vanity and therefore should be shunned. According to Bach's biographer Jan Chiapusso, Frohne 'was guilty of thwarting the genius in his endeavors of art and religious conscience . . . the church and its pastor refused Bach's every attempt to use his great musical gifts for their services of worship'. This is probably too unkind to Frohne, who was no more conservative than many clergy of his time and may have seen Bach less as a genius than as an opinionated youth who failed in loyalty to his own church. At any rate, he and his organist could not see eye to eye, and matters were not helped when Bach composed for the rival Marienkirche. Nor was Frohne happy when Pastor Eilmar became a friend of the young couple and later, in December 1708, the godfather of their first child, Catharina Dorothea.

Eilmar provided the texts for Bach's cantata No. 71, *Gott ist mein König*. This was a brilliant celebratory piece composed for a semi-secular occasion, the inauguration of Mühlhausen's new city council on February 4, 1708. The day was festive throughout, with a procession of forty-eight robed dignitaries from the city hall to the Marienkirche, where the cantata was performed by solo voices, a choir and an orchestra that included three trumpets and drums as well as the usual wind, strings and organ. The whole day ended with a banquet and the consumption of a huge cake made

Copperplate engraving of Mülhausen, by Matthäus Merian

by local bakers. As for the new cantata, the city council liked it so much that they had it printed.

But all was not so well at the Blasiuskirche. Apart from his uneasy relations with Pastor Frohne, Bach was dissatisfied with the organ and told the church council in February 1708 that it needed repairs and additions. In the same month he drew up a specification of his requirements, which they considered and accepted. Yet this was not enough to content him; he may already have been thinking of moving on again, and four months later he resigned. Before doing so, he did two things. One was to write another church cantata (No. 196) for the wedding on June 5 of Pastor Stauber to Maria Barbara's aunt Regina Wedemann, and the other was to audition successfully as an organist for the court of Duke Wilhelm Ernst of Weimar.

He was now ready to leave Mühlhausen, and from the letter of resignation that he wrote to his church council on June 25 it is clear that, at twenty-five, neither his ambition nor his prickly temperament had been subdued. Indeed, his resignation letter, in which he proudly mentioned his invitation to the Weimar court, was bluntly critical. He complained that at the Blasiuskirche he had been prevented from honoring God with proper music; that he had suffered hindrance and vexation; that performances in nearby villages in which he had sometimes taken part often surpassed that of his own church; that he had maintained the organ in the face of opposition; that he had spent his own money on music for the church's library, and finally that his salary was insufficient despite his simple lifestyle. At Weimar, he declared, he would at last be able 'to pursue the ultimate aim of properly conceived church music'.

It says something for the church council that they did not dismiss the letter as arrogant. Instead, they tried to persuade Bach to withdraw it and only accepted it with reluctance 'since he could not be made to stay'. They seem to have recognized the justice of Bach's strictures, and in return he offered them his services in continuing to supervise the rebuilding and repair work on the Blasiuskirche organ. A year later, the council paid him to return to Mühlhausen to take part in a Reformation festival. He must have composed music for this and another such festival in 1710, but it has been lost. He also probably inaugurated the rebuilt organ when it was completed in 1709, and may have composed his famous organ chorale *Ein' feste Burg ist unser Gott* BWV720 (a tune adapted by Luther himself) for the occasion.

He was succeeded at the Blasiuskirche by his cousin Johann Friedrich Bach, slightly older than himself and the third son of his Eisenstadt uncle Johann Christoph Bach. It must have seemed to people in the region that the Bach family were everywhere as far as music was concerned. J. F. Bach's appointment proved much longer-lasting, for he remained at Mühlhausen until his death in 1730.

Although Bach's point in his resignation letter, that moving to Weimar would allow him to pursue his higher aims for church music, is an indication of his musical ideals, it was hardly the whole story, for his salary at Weimar was to be 150 guilders a year, nearly twice what he received at Mühlhausen. In 1711 it was to rise again by fifty guilders and three years later, when he was appointed Konzertmeister to the Weimar court, it became 250, five times what he had earned on beginning work at Arnstadt a decade earlier. In fact, Bach knew that by going to Weimar he was bettering himself and accepting a position of prestige. He also knew fairly accurately what musical prospects the new appointment would offer. In his own words to his church council, he was receiving 'the most gracious admission of His Serene Highness of Saxe-Weimar into his Court Kapelle and Chamber Music'.

The word *Kapelle* means chapel, but in those days it commonly meant an instrumental or vocal ensemble, so that Bach's description of his new job might seem unconnected with church music. But he knew that he could expect to play the organ for religious services in the ducal chapel, a place of importance to the devout Duke Wilhelm Ernst. The most powerful figure in Weimar, he had ruled for some years with his younger brother Duke Johann Ernst, in accordance with a family law established in the previous century. However, the music-loving Johann Ernst had died fairly young, in 1707, leaving the court in the care of the serious-minded Wilhelm, childless and a divorcee. He, too, appreciated music and it was he who had offered Bach his new post after hearing him play. There was a younger generation at court in the persons of Johann Ernst's two sons, of whom the elder, Ernst August, was to attain his majority in 1709; but although he then became co-regent, his uncle effectively remained in charge.

During Bach's stay at Weimar five years before, he had struck up a friendship with the court's elderly organist Johann Effler and had almost certainly sometimes deputized for him. Now, Effler needed the help of a younger man all the more and, indeed, on being appointed on July 14, 1708, Bach received the title of *Hoforganist*, court organist. Effler may have had a hand in this, for he knew that he could not continue much longer. In December 1709, an 'old, sick servant', he retired and died just two years later. Bach therefore expected to become a central figure of the Weimar court, both as an organist and as a chamber musician (*Cammermusikus*) who played the harpsichord, violin or viola in an orchestra. As far as we know, his expectations were justified and his new appointment proved congenial to him. He and Maria Barbara were to remain at Weimar until 1717, and six of their children were born there, beginning with Catharina Dorothea in December 1708.

A romanticised imaginary picture of
the Bach family at morning prayer (Toby Rosenthal, 1870)

Weimar

Since Bach had been brought up as a devout Lutheran who saw his art as serving God, it may seem that now, aged twenty-five, he had become worldly in leaving his career as a church organist to serve a secular ruler. At that time, however, such a ruler was seen as God's representative, governing men's worldly affairs just as the church attended to their immortal souls. Every court had its chapel and strict religious observances. In Weimar's case this was especially so, for Duke Wilhelm Ernst had studied theology and sometimes questioned his servants about the sermons they heard at Sunday services, where attendance was compulsory. Nevertheless, things were done in the grand manner, as befitted a leading ducal court, and Bach knew that he need fear no austerity or penny-pinching. There was even an elderly resident poet, Johann Christoph Lorbeer, whose works, much approved of by the duke for their moral tone, included *Lob der edlen Musik*, 'The Praise of Noble Music', while another man of letters, the court librarian Salomo Franck, was to collaborate with Bach in the composition of church cantatas.

Thus Weimar's court musicians had their importance, although they were still servants and strictly governed in many matters, such as their dress (Bach must have worn livery). As for the music that Bach composed here, it was supposed to have qualities of harmony, dignity and propriety, reflecting the properly governed state which Weimar was considered to be. As his biographer Hannsdieter Wohlfarth has put it, 'God's creation was still understood as a well-ordered community', and he quotes the philosopher Leibniz, a contemporary of Bach and a courtier himself: 'Because the universe as a whole is fully ordered by God, so complete order must rule in each

The Schloss Belvedere,
Weimar

individual being.' The intellectual climate was such that people were not expected to question the existing social order, and although new ideals of human brotherhood, freedom and equality were now awakening in Europe, no one in this part of Germany could voice them without risking his career and perhaps his liberty. Bach, however, was no revolutionary, and from his point of view the life of the Weimar court was rich. Duke Wilhelm had reinstated its Kapelle, a flexible body of musicians with a dozen or so instrumentalists, including string players and trumpeters, sometimes supplemented by military bandsmen, and several singers, including choirboys. Some of these musicians were versatile and could take on more than one role: for example, one of the tenors, Johann Döbernitz, also played the bassoon. The Kapellmeister, or overall director of music, was Johann Samuel Drese, who had been at the court for some years. He was assisted by his son Johann Wilhelm, an arrangement which, while sounding unsatisfactorily nepotistic, worked well enough. However, neither Drese possessed outstanding gifts, and the father was now well into his sixties, so that Johann Wilhelm seems to have taken on some of his duties. As in the case of the organist Effler, here was a situation where Bach could bide his time and hope for promotion; and probably his noble employer thought on similar lines.

Bach's duties do not seem to have been onerous. He played the organ in the Himmelsburg, as the ducal chapel was called, and took part in chamber music, but this still left time for other things. A pupil from Mühlhausen, Johann Martin Schubart, came to Weimar to study with him and was later to succeed him as court organist. In due course he also acquired other pupils; amongst whom were Johann Caspar Vogler (who in turn succeeded Schubart) and Johann Tobias Krebs. He also now taught two young relatives, Johann Lorenz Bach and his Ohrdruf nephew Johann Bernhard Bach, the latter then being a boy who would eventually succeed his father

Johann Christoph Bach as organist of the Michaeliskirche in Ohrdruf.

Bach continued to pursue his interest in organ building, an area of knowledge in which his skill was now widely valued. He was also paid in 1709, and again in 1710, for repairing harpsichords belonging to the sons of the late Duke Johann Ernst. At this time, when a great deal of organ building and rebuilding was being undertaken in Germany, he was often consulted and seems to have freely given advice and encouragement. When an organ builder named Nicolaus Trebs, whom he had known at Mühlhausen, was invited to construct a new instrument at Taubach, a village near Weimar, he asked Bach to make out its specification and test it on its completion in 1710. In his turn, Bach liked Trebs and in a testimonial written the following year, called him 'a reasonable and conscientious man' – sober eighteenth-century words that nevertheless implied high praise. He then invited Trebs to work on the Weimar organ in the Himmelsburg, which with its two

Arcangelo Corelli (1653–1713) an early master of the concerto form

manuals and twenty-five stops was a small instrument compared to some that Bach had heard and played in Hamburg and Lübeck; it was also smaller than the one at the Blasiuskirche in Mühlhausen. Between 1712 and 1714, and under Bach's supervision, Trebs set about making improvements and additions and seems to have given satisfaction. In November 1713, Bach invited Trebs to be a godfather to his son Johann Gottfried.

Another friend was the organist of Weimar's Stadtkirche, Johann Gottfried Walther. He and Bach were rleated through a maternal grandfather, and when he and his wife had a son in 1712, Bach agreed to be a godfather. They shared an interest in Italian music and Walther introduced Bach to works by such contemporary masters of the concerto form as Corelli and Vivaldi, whose music Bach then sometimes arranged for organ. It seems that Walther once challenged Bach's boast that he could play any organ music at sight by presenting him with something virtually impossible which defeated him. Their relationship did not suffer, as was once thought, but the story is significant because there is little doubt that even Bach's friends sometimes wanted to dent his high opinion of his own remarkable gifts.

It is not known where Bach and his growing family lived during these Weimar years, except that he does not seem to have stayed in the castle itself. This was actually a distinction, since most of those in the duke's employment were required to do so. Even the Kapellmeister, Drese, lived there and was allowed to draw from the kitchen a daily loaf of bread and measure of beer. However, we know that in March 1709 Bach and his wife, together with a sister of hers, were lodging with the court singer and 'master of the pages', Adam Immanuel Weldig. It is likely that they stayed there until the summer of 1713, when Weldig left Weimar to take up another post. But they kept in touch, and Weldig was to be a godfather of Carl Philipp Emanuel Bach, born on

March 8, 1714. This boy was destined to be the most famous Bach after his father, a man admired by both Haydn and Mozart for opening up the way to new forms and feelings in music. Another of his godfathers was the distinguished musician Georg Philipp Telemann, a former Kapellmeister at Eisenach.

Although Bach seems to have been content enough at Weimar, in the last months of 1713, after five years there, he once again considered a move. He visited the university town of Halle, Handel's birthplace, and heard of the death of the Liebfrauenkirche organist Friedrich Wilhelm Zachow, Handel's teacher. The instrument that Zachow had played was about to be enlarged, and Bach was tempted. It seems that the pastor, Juhann Michael Heineccius, pressed Bach to apply for the post and that he did so, composing a cantata in support of his application which may have been his No. 63, *Christen, ätzet diesen Tag*, possibly with a text by Heineccius.

Handel in 1750,
by Georg Friedrich Schmidt
(copperplate engraving)

On December 14, he was offered a contract, but by then he was having second thoughts, not least because the basic salary of 171 thalers was less than he earned at Weimar. A month later he wrote back to Halle enquiring closely as to the additional perquisites of wedding fees and the like (the *Accidentien*) which traditionally added to an organist's salary, as they often do today. His prospective employers replied that while these should be substantial, they could make no guarantees, and asked him to make up his mind. It is almost certain that he then went to Duke Wilhelm, for on March 2, 1714, 'at his most humble request', he was promoted to Konzertmeister, ranking below the Vice-Kapellmeister J. W. Drese but now third among Weimar's court musicians, at an annual salary of 250 florins. (There were several currencies in Germany at this time, but the guilder, thaler and florin seem to have had roughly the same value.) After this, he formally refused the Halle post.

Not surprisingly, some people felt that Bach had used Halle as a lever to improve his position at Weimar, and he found himself on rather shaky ground morally, if not legally. The Liebfrauenkirche council instructed their lawyer August Becker to pursue the matter. But in a letter to Becker dated March 19, 1714, Bach denied that he had actively sought the post at Halle ('as I see it, I allowed my name to go forward'), and added sharply that 'no one can be expected to move to a place where he will be worse off . . . it should not be concluded from all this that I have deceived the worshipful Collegium so as to persuade my gracious master to increase my salary; he already holds my service and my art in such regard that there is no need for me to travel to Halle in order to improve my salary here. I am sorry then, that what the worshipful Collegium was so certain of has turned out so uncertainly.' Fortunately, this explanation was accepted and he made his peace with Halle. In April 1716, he and two other well-known organists were invited to the Liebfrauenkirche to examine and

Bach at the age of thirty, painted by Johann Ernst Reutsch

inaugurate the new organ there, receiving a substantial fee and expenses for the days that they spent in the city.

Bach soon knew that he had made the right decision in staying at Weimar, for in March 1715, Duke Wilhelm ordered that his Konzertmeister should receive a share of the perquisites and honoraria earned by the Kapelle. In effect, he was being recognized as a deputy Kapellmeister. Furthermore, his salary now exceeded that of Kapellmeister Drese, perhaps because he now composed a cantata each month for performance in the Himmelsburg. The first of these cantatas was No. 182 (as usual, the numbers bear no relation to dates of composition), *Himmelskönig, sei willkommen*, and it was first performed on Palm Sunday 1714, not long after he took up his new appointment.

However, of the works Bach composed while at Weimar, the most important are those which he wrote for the organ. Thirty-nine major organ pieces date from these years, 1708–17, more than he wrote in the three decades that remained to him after he left the city. They include his noble Passacaglia in C minor, BWV582, and numerous preludes, toccatas, fantasias and fugues. Here, it is has been said, are works that 'stand as eternal monuments, profoundly expressive of deep, ecstatic spiritual experience . . . while still burning with his ardent fire of youth'. There are also pieces based on chorale melodies, including several which make up a set called the *Orgel-Büchlein* or 'Little Organ Book', BWV599–644, wittily inscribed as for 'a beginner at the organ' and also 'in praise of the Almighty's will, and for my neighbor's greater skill'. The words may seem curious, but were probably not false modesty, for Bach never stopped learning and, encouraged by his colleague Walther, studied Italian organ music by such men as Frescobaldi, Albinoni, and Bonporti and made copies of it for himself. He wrote other keyboard pieces for the harpsichord, including his six English Suites, BWV806–11, and numerous arrangements of violin concertos by Vivaldi, the Italian composer most admired by the young Duke Johann Ernst, who then played them for himself. Bach also made two-handed arrangements of two concertos by Johann Ernst himself and one of a violin concerto by Telemann.

*Telemann,
in a copperplate
engraving of 1744
by Georg Lichtensteger*

Among the cantatas from Bach's Weimar years is the secular 'Hunt' Cantata, *Was mir behagt, ist nur die muntre Jagd*, BWV208, a delightfully vigorous piece composed for the birthday of Duke Christian of Saxe-Weissenfels in 1713, which includes the tactfully loyal sentiment, 'Where the sovereign ruleth wisely, joy and peace the land have blessed.' This had words by Salomo Franck, as did the church cantatas Nos. 12, 31, 132, 152, 155, 161, 162, 165, 185 and almost certainly others. Together these two men made the Lutheran church cantata into something shapely and colorful, even dramatic, with operatic devices such as recitatives and arias married to specially written texts that paraphrased biblical ones or otherwise expressed pious sentiments. In later life, writing cantatas with another poet, Picander, Bach recommended Franck to him as a model of style.

However, Bach's production of cantatas fluctuated after the beginning of 1716, with none dating from most of that year and then three coming in quick succession at its end. All of these are lost in their original form, although we have revisions of them that Bach made in 1723. This may have been because he seems, at this time, to have given his services increasingly to the young co-regent, Duke Ernst August, who occupied a part of the Wilhelmsburg called the Rotes Schloss, or Red Castle. Ernst August's brother Johann Ernst had also lived there until chronic illness made him leave Weimar in 1714 (he died in the following year), and, as we have seen, Bach had shared his passion for the Italian music that he brought back from his studies at Utrecht University in 1711–3. With his untimely death so soon after this, Bach must have felt a deep sense of loss and, as a result, was all the more loyal to his brother Ernst August. Unfortunately, there was some ill-feeling between the young duke and his gloomy uncle, Wilhelm, and at one stage Wilhelm even imposed fines on members of his household who provided services for his nephew. Bach seems to have defied the disapproval of his employer and joined in a presentation to Ernst August on the occasion of his marriage to a sister of Prince Leopold of Anhalt-Cöthen in January 1716. And he also gave another performance of his 'Hunt' Cantata for the young duke's birthday three months later.

Because of this, and perhaps for other reasons of which we know nothing, relations between Bach and his employer deteriorated, matters coming to a head when Kapellmeister Drese died in December 1716. Since his son was not greatly gifted, Bach hoped strongly for promotion as the aged Drese's successor, and his composition of three cantatas in the month of Drese's death may have represented his vigorous bid for the appointment. Instead, Duke Wilhelm snubbed him not once but twice, first by inviting Telemann to accept the post and then, when Telemann declined, by offering it to the younger Drese, who naturally accepted at once.

Duke Wilhelm had thus made it crystal clear to Bach that his prospects of promotion at Weimar were closed, and once again he started to look for another post. But now he wanted nothing less than the position of Kapellmeister, and very soon he found the prospect of one at the court of Prince Leopold of Anhalt-Cöthen, Duke Ernst August's brother-in-law. Leopold may have been present at his sister's recent Weimar wedding, to which Bach had contributed music; alternatively, she may have given good reports of him. Whatever the case, the existing leader of the Cöthen Kapelle, Augustin Retinae Stricker, was reaching the end of his three-year contract, and by the beginning of August the Prince had invited Bach to replace him at a salary of 400 thalers, about a third more than he was paid at Weimar. He even started paying Bach's salary at once.

But he and Bach had both reckoned without Duke Wilhelm. Perhaps suspecting his nephew's hand in all this, he flatly refused to let Bach go and attempted to sweeten the pill by allowing him to travel to Dresden, probably in September, and then setting up an endowment fund for all his court musicians to mark his birthday on October 30. Bach remained unimpressed, but was still at Weimar when the birthday and the bicentenary of the Reformation were marked by three days of festivities. They must have included music, yet as far as we know he composed no cantata for the occasion, and this may have seemed like insubordination to his employer, who was, after all, a near-absolute ruler who expected to have his way.

However, Duke Wilhelm, like others before him, was up against Bach's characteristic stubbornness. For a while there was a stalemate, during which he might have realized that he could gain nothing by keeping his employee against his will. But Bach became impatient, and evidently demanded his release so forcefully that Wilhelm had him confined to his quarters from November 6 (some accounts even use the word 'imprisoned'). Whether this was supposed to make Bach give in or simply intended as a humiliation, it made no difference: he was determined to leave and eventually Duke Wilhelm admitted defeat. But it was in disgrace and without ceremony that Bach and his family left Weimar for Cöthen on December 2, 1717.

Cöthen

Though Bach was exchanging one court for another, Cöthen had a very different ruler. Prince Leopold was a young man, born nine years after Bach in 1694. Like Bach, he had suffered the childhood loss of his father; he also showed musical talent, and at thirteen persuaded his widowed mother to employ court musicians with whom he could perform. Before he was twenty he had traveled widely, visiting England among other countries, and had become a skilled player of stringed instruments and the harpsichord. He also developed a good bass voice. On reaching the age of twenty-one in 1715, he formed a Kapelle of his own at Cöthen, calling it his *collegium musicum*. By 1716 it amounted to eighteen instrumentalists, playing strings, wind and keyboard.

Cöthen (now spelt Köthen), situated to the north of Halle, was, and remains, a smallish town, and Bach must have found the court atmosphere more congenial than the chilly grandeur of Duke Wilhelm's court at Weimar. Prince Leopold's palace was in the town center but, surrounded by a moat and well-tended gardens, it was an island of privileged comfort and culture set apart from the commoners' world. As at Weimar, Bach and his family seem to have lodged outside the castle, but it is not known where. Tradition has placed them in the Wallstrasse, but it now seems more likely that they lived first at 11 Stiftstrasse and then at 12 Holzmarkt.

Bach arrived in Cöthen in the first week of December 1717, in time to join in celebrations for the Prince's birthday on the tenth, and may have hastily written a cantata or other new piece, since the court accounts suggest that something was performed. Leopold evidently gave his new Kapellmeister some freedom, for only a week after this, he traveled to Leipzig to test an organ newly built by Johann Scheibe for the Paulinuskirche, the university church; however, this is the only work of that kind that he seems to have done during his six years at Cöthen.

It was at Cöthen that Maria Barbara Bach gave birth to the last of her seven children, a son born on November 17, 1718. He was named Leopold Augustus, and it was a mark of the Prince's regard for Bach that he agreed to be a godfather to the child who took his name and that the christening took place in the court chapel. Unfortunately, the boy was to die before his first birthday.

Although Bach had left Weimar from time to time on business, he traveled still more from Cöthen, and further afield. This was partly because the prince himself was often on the move: in May and June of 1718, for example, Bach and five of his musicians attended Leopold during his annual summer sojourn at the popular spa town of Carlsbad, some considerable distance to the south. Early in 1719, Bach went alone on another long trip, this time north to Berlin to purchase a new harpsichord for his Kapelle. (It may have been here or in Carlsbad that he met the Margrave Christian Ludwig of Brandenburg, to whom he was later to dedicate his Brandenburg Concertos.) It was for this instrument, a large two manual one by a Berlin maker called Michael Mietke, that he wrote the important solo part in the Fifth Brandenburg Concerto, completed two years later, and almost certainly he played it at the first performance of the work, which took place at Cöthen.

In the same year Bach made the first of two unsuccessful efforts to meet his great contemporary Handel, now resident in England. Born in the same year, they had gone different ways, for while Bach had traveled relatively little, Handel was already a cosmopolitan and equally at home in Italian opera and English odes. Like every musician, Bach knew of his outstanding gifts – he was, for example, equally at home in Italian opera and English odes – and, on hearing that he was visiting Halle, his

*Portrait of
Prince Leopold
of Anhalt-Cöthen,
in half-armour
with a black boy
as attendant,
anonymous and undated*

birthplace just twenty miles away, set off by coach to visit him. He arrived only to find that Handel had left earlier the same day. Ten years later, something similar was to happen: Handel came again to Halle, but Bach, now in Leipzig and unwell, sent his son Wilhelm Friedemann to ask his colleague to visit him. Unfortunately, Handel was unable to do so, and Bach was grieved never to have met 'this truly great man of whom he thought so highly'.

Apart from this disappointment, these early years at Cöthen were happy ones. Still in his thirties, Bach held the highest musical rank then available as a Kapellmeister, for he was answerable only to his employer and wholly in charge of court music. His salary equaled that of the court's highest officers. His duties seem to have been light, consisting mainly of performing with his small orchestra (Kapelle) and composing music for this or that courtly occasion. The only drawback was that the court organ was a small, two-manual one with just thirteen stops, but that does not seem to have worried him too much, although he now composed little organ music. As at Weimar, he also had pupils, among them perhaps the prince himself. All in all, these were conditions that favored creativity and contentment, and perhaps for the first time he found himself at ease both with his employer and with the musicians who played and sang under his direction. His own description of Cöthen in later life sums it up: 'There I had a gracious prince, who both loved and knew music, and in his service I intended to spend the rest of my life.'

However, his circumstances were soon to change, for in 1720 he lost his wife and in the following year Prince Leopold married a lady who had no interest in music. In May 1720, Leopold went again to take the waters at Carlsbad and took Bach with him. But this time he stayed longer than the five weeks or so of earlier visits, and was still there in July. In the meantime, Maria Barbara Bach died and was buried on July 7. The cause of her death is not recorded: it may have been in childbirth, though a sudden summer fever seems more likely, since their son Carl Philipp Emanuel later wrote of his mother's 'illness'. No news of her death reached Bach in Carlsbad. It is possible that the Cöthen officials failed to send word to him, but more likely that the Prince and his staff were leaving for home at about the same time. Thus, having left his wife in good health, Bach returned to find her buried. As Carl Philipp Emanuel Bach later wrote, 'The news that she had been ill and died reached him only when he entered his own house.' She was only thirty-five.

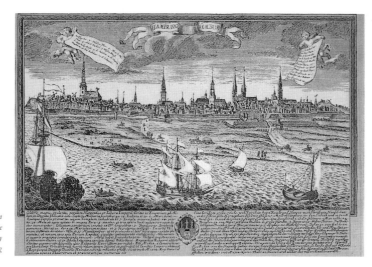

Hamburg in 1700, copperplate engraving by Michael Wening

Bach's biographer Malcolm Boyd has suggested that this was such a blow to him that 'life at Cöthen, which until then had been the happiest he had known, must now have become distasteful'. But that seems too black-and-white a way of looking at it. After all, like everyone of his time, he was familiar with premature death, for he and his wife had lost four of their seven children. His thirteen years of marriage to Maria Barbara had been 'blissful', according to the later testimony of their son Carl Philipp Emanuel, but although he mourned, he was too rational and active a man to give in to self-pitying, protracted grief.

Even so, his wife's death did unsettle him, and may have made him think that, after a dozen years of court service in Weimar and Cöthen, he ought now to return to the kind of church post for which his Lutheran schooling had fitted him so well and which he had sought at the start of his career. Two months after his bereavement, he may have applied for a vacant organist's post at the Jacobikirche in Hamburg, where there was a fine, relatively new four-manual organ with sixty stops. Although no correspondence exists proving an application, he did visit Hamburg and by November 21 his name was one of eight being considered by the church council, which could only have happened with his consent. One attraction the post had for him was that the pastor of the Jacobikirche, Erdmann Neumeister, was a friend and had written some of his cantata texts; another may have been that it offered educational and other facilities for his three motherless sons, and he may have remembered his own upbringing in a church school and all it had given him.

Although he did not attend the official auditions planned by the Jakobikirche council, returning to Cöthen just before they began on November 28, he seems to have been heard, for during his visit to Hamburg he played the Jacobikirche organ and two others by the same maker, Arp Schnitger, that were in the Nikolaikirche and

Bach as Kapellmeister
at Cöthen,
a portrait dating from 1720
by Johann Jakob Ihle

Johanniskirche. What appears to have been his formal audition took place in the Catharinenkirche, where he played for over two hours before city officials and an interested public. However, the listener who meant most to him was the church's own organist, J. A. Reincken, whom he had heard there as a Lüneburg schoolboy. Reincken had held this post for over sixty years and was now an unbelievable ninety-seven. Bach had heard him improvise, on this same organ, on the chorale melody 'By the Waters of Babylon', and now someone asked Bach to take the same melody as the basis for an extemporization. After he had played for nearly half an hour, using a succession of styles to cumulative effect, the aged Reincken was deeply moved, saying, 'I thought that this art had perished, but I see that it still lives in you.'

Bach was strongly placed for the Jacobikirche post, for three other candidates did not attend for auditions and the remaining four did not meet the council's expectations. It was formally offered to him, and by December 12 the church council was awaiting his reply. However, he now refused it and the post was given instead to a little-known organist called Johann Joachim Heitmann, an appointment that had as much to do with the age-old practice of simony (the sale of church appointments) as with artistic talent. The Jacobikirche council had actually stated that, at the time of appointment, while musical ability was the chief consideration, the chosen candidate might 'of his own free will give a token of his gratitude' which the church could accept and use as needed. When it became known that Heitmann, on being appointed, had presented the church with a substantial sum (4,000 marks), someone described him scornfully as using cash better than his fingers, while Pastor Neumeister thundered that 'if an angel from Bethlehem came from heaven and played divinely but had no money, he would have to fly away again'. Bach must have known of this unsavory aspect of the appointment, and it may have made him abandon the idea of moving. It has also been suggested that he had hoped, if appointed, to become the overall director of music in this great Hanseatic city, but realized that this would not happen. Although the matter of the Jacobikirche came to nothing, Bach's scrupulous honesty and directness would not have let him conceal his plans from his employer, and it says something for this kindly young nobleman that he was prepared, however reluctantly, to let his treasured Kapellmeister go. He must, however, have been glad when Bach abandoned the idea of the Hamburg position.

Thus, at the end of 1720, it seemed that Bach would remain at Cöthen for the forseeable future, with congenial work and a sympathetic employer. Yet he must have found life difficult as a widower with three young sons to care for; the boys were now aged ten (Wilhelm Friedemann), six (Carl Philipp Emanuel) and five (Johann Gottfried Bernhard). However, nothing is known of how he coped domestically, since his first biographers, writing well after his death and mainly interested in his music, recorded little about his personal affairs.

This was the time of the completion of the six Brandenburg Concertos, BWV1046–51, dedicated to the Margrave of Brandenburg in fulsome French and dated March 24, 1721. English biographers usually quote Bach as saying that he 'took a couple of years' over their composition, but the German phrase *ein paar Jahre* means 'a few years' or even 'some years', and he actually composed them over a period of about a decade, with Nos. 3 and 6 being written in Weimar and the latter possibly dating back to 1708. The others probably date from his four Cöthen years, with No. 5, the last to be composed, being written for the Mietke harpsichord that he had acquired in Berlin. The odd thing about this apparent commission from a nobleman, however, is that, as far as is known, Bach received no fee, nor even a letter of thanks. Indeed, the margrave seems to have accepted the music very casually. Perhaps he knew that these pieces, fine though they were, had not been composed especially for him or his court, which in fact did not have the musicians to perform them. When he died and some of his effects were disposed of, the manuscripts of these concertos were seen not to have been used. But Bach undoubtedly performed them at Cöthen, joining his musicians in bringing them to life.

These Brandenburg Concertos are joyful works which sum up the orchestral side of Bach's art at this stage of his career, when he was in his mid-thirties and at the height of his powers. They are not concertos in the modern sense of works for a single soloist in dialogue, or conflict, with a full symphony orchestra, but works for smaller groups of instruments with individual or group solos as needed; another, more accurate, term for such music is *concerto grosso*. Thus, although the harpsichord is prominent in No. 5 and the trumpet features strongly in No. 2, they are not the only soloists in these pieces, and No. 3 is for three violas, three violas da gamba and three cellos (plus keyboard continuo) and has no soloist at all, although the groups exchange ideas with each other. Nor is the number of movements fixed: No. 1 has four movements, No. 2 three, and No. 3 just two linked by a single bar of two slow chords. These works embody Bach's flexible views as to musical form and also the fact that in his time the word 'concerto' often simply meant music for several instruments playing as an ensemble. His own title for the pieces was *Concerts avec plusieurs instruments*.

Two other orchestral works from the Cöthen years are the first and last of four suites, BWV1066–9. Again these are in several movements but are more expansive than the concertos. All four offer ceremonial yet genial music; however, the Third Suite, with its famous slow melody that later acquired the name 'Air on the G string' (Bach's title is merely 'Air'), was written, like the Second, after the composer left Cöthen for Leipzig.

It was also at Cöthen that Bach wrote most of his chamber music, that is, music for just three or four players rather than a bigger ensemble. There are two trio sonatas, one for two flutes and harpsichord and the other for violin, oboe and harpsichord, plus six sonatas for violin and harpsichord and others for flute. In addition, he composed six sonatas and partitas, BWV1001–6, for unaccompanied violin. The difference between the two forms resembles that between concertos and suites: sonatas and concertos are more formal and alternate slow and fast movements, while a partita or suite has a sequence of dance movements. At the time when Bach was composing, the dances normally used were the allemande, courante, sarabande and gigue, and they all feature in his six suites for unaccompanied violin, BWV1007–12. However, in Bach's hands the form was flexible and he added other dances to these suites, namely minuets in Nos. 1 and 2, bourrées in Nos. 2 and 3, and gavottes in Nos. 3 and 4. As a practical man, he must have had a player in mind when composing such pieces as these, where the artistic and technical difficulties are of a high order, but we do not know who he was.

He also composed keyboard music, some of it for his son and pupil Wilhelm Friedemann. It was for him that he composed, section by section, what he called a *Clavier-Büchlein für Wilhelm Friedemann Bach*, which begins with an explanation of notation and ornaments and goes on to practice basic fingerwork. The Two-part and Three-part Inventions, BWV772–86 and 787–801, fifteen of each, also belong in this collection: each is in a single movement and the names refer to the number of contrapuntal parts or 'voices' involved. Wilhelm Friedemann ('Friede', as his father affectionately called him) must have made rapid progress, something which his teacher probably took for granted, for the collection came to include some of the preludes in what was to be one of Bach's greatest keyboard works, the first book of the *Well-Tempered Clavier* (or Forty-Eight Preludes and Fugues), BWV846–69, which dates from

1722 and uses all the major and minor keys in turn. Bach seems to have been a patient and methodical teacher who liked his work, at least with intelligent and diligent pupils. He did not force them (there were others too at this time), but gently guided them through the basics of notation and keyboard work. In the foreword to the Two-part and Three-part Inventions, he wrote that here was 'a clear way' to play in two and three parts and 'to attain a singing style in playing and also to gain a strong sense of composition'. Technique was never an end in itself, but always had to serve music.

In 1722, Bach was to begin another *Büchlein*, this time for a new member of the family, for on December 3, 1721, almost exactly two years after his wife's death, he remarried. Anna Magdalena Wilcke was just twenty, the daughter of a musician and briefly a *Sängerin* (singer) at the nearby court of Anhalt-Zerbst; she must have played an instrument, too, since she was described as a *Musicantin* (musician). Bach knew the court and may have met her there, and she may have sung at Cöthen as a visitor. It seems that he then brought her to Cöthen on a more permanent basis, for she was described as 'a court singer here' when, on September 25, both she and Bach became godparents to the son of Prince Leopold's butler Christian Hahn. Bach did not insist on her giving up her Cöthen post when they married, for he valued her skills and her salary was useful. She, in turn, may have enjoyed being able to continue in her profession, and helped her husband by proving to be a neat and accurate copyist of his music. Prince Leopold must have welcomed the marriage since it would help to keep his Kapellmeister at Cöthen, and he gave Bach permission to marry in his own home. To help the celebrations, the happy bridegroom visited the town's cellars to buy Rhine wine at a discount price of twenty per cent.

Autograph title page of Bach's Clavierbüchlein *for his son Wilhelm Friedrich Bach, 1720*

Clavier - Büchlein.

vor

Wilhelm Friedemann Bach.

angefangen in

Cöthen den

22. Januar

Ao. 1720.

Soon after the marriage, Bach began providing Anna Magdalena with keyboard pieces, some of which are agreeably light in style while others are more challenging. She seems to have been a good woman and a good companion, and Bach knew that if he should die she would be a mother to her stepchildren (she herself was to give him thirteen more children). He even wrote lines to this effect alongside some of the music that he composed for her, as well as a short love poem ending: 'O how with joy my heart is filled / To see your beauty blooming, / Till all my soul with music's thrilled, / My heart's with joy o'erflowing.' The text of a little song – 'Bist du bei mir' – that he composed for her says that, should he die, he can 'go with joy, the fingers of your loving hand my eyelids gently closing'. These words give us a rare glimpse into the heart of a musician who usually preferred to express himself through his art. Incidentally, a further insight into his domestic life is provided by another, humorous, poem which says how a pipe and good tobacco pleasingly passes the time. It seems that Bach was a smoker!

Thus, at the time of Bach's second marriage all seemed to augur well for his future at Cöthen, and the receipt of a legacy of 500 guilders, expected at the time of the wedding but delayed by legal wrangles, was a welcome bonus. However, a cloud over this happiness emerged from a quite unexpected quarter. Just after his marriage, Prince Leopold also married, choosing as his bride his cousin, the Princess Friderica of Anhalt-Bernburg. Their wedding took place at Bernburg, but when they returned to Cöthen, there were further lengthy celebrations. These perhaps passed off well, but it soon became clear to Bach that the court atmosphere was changing. The princess, as he was later to tell his old friend Georg Erdmann, proved to be 'a-musa'. (This Latin word is hard to translate, although a modern dictionary defines 'amusia' as 'the inability to comprehend or produce musical sounds'.) What he must have meant was that the princess was unmusical, uninterested in music or simply resentful of her husband's passion for an activity in which she played no part. He may therefore have seen her as unfriendly and a danger to his excellent relations with his employer. It is possible, however, that she was unhappy at Cöthen, or even unwell. Bach could not have foreseen it, but she was to die in April 1723 after just over a year of marriage.

Accordingly, and probably with sadness, Bach began again to think of leaving Cöthen for a new post, and this time his thoughts turned towards Leipzig, a city of 30,000 inhabitants where the Kantor of the Thomasschule, Johann Kuhnau, had died on June 5, 1722. Kuhnau's post involved the direction of the music at the city's principal churches and was one of the most important in that

The Thomaskirche, Leipzig, engraving by Joachim Ernst Scheffler

part of Germany. The council of the Thomaskirche met on July 14 to consider the question of his successor, and several musicians put their names forward, including Bach's old friend Telemann and some others already known to him as colleagues. Telemann, now based in Hamburg, was offered the appointment on August 13 and accepted, but his existing employers then offered him better pay and conditions and he withdrew. On November 23 and December 21 the Thomaskirche council met again and considered five further candidates, who by this time included Bach, but then settled on Johann Christoph Graupner, a former Thomasschule pupil now working as a Kapellmeister at Darmstadt. But he, too, changed his mind on being offered a better deal by his current employers. While the appointment remained in the balance, the council played safe and left the door open to the other candidates, inviting Bach to perform two new cantatas for them on February 7 in the Thomaskirche. When Graupner sent his refusal in April and recommended Bach, the council offered the post to him provided that he gained his release from Cöthen. All was agreed quickly, although one councilor hoped that the new man's music 'would not be theatrical'.

The story has often been told that a member of Bach's appointing committee said during these deliberations that 'since the best cannot be had we must accept the mediocre', an indication that the church worthies quite failed to recognize Bach's genius. However, the truth is that this councilor, Abraham Christoph Platz, was grouping among 'the best' (plural) Telemann, Graupner and Bach himself because all were unwilling or unable to teach Latin to the Thomasschule's choristers (as required of the Kantor) and it looked as if they might have to appoint an ordinary music teacher. The problem lay in the unrealistic job specification, which required a church musician who was also a pedagogue. Bach resolved the matter of teaching Latin by offering to pay a deputy to do this chore for which he was unfitted. He was later to wish that he had not been so generous.

The final stage of the negotiations took place at Cöthen and must have been painful. Bach obtained his release in the very month in which the prince's wife died. Had it not been for his marriage, Leopold would probably have kept Bach's services. As it was, he had lost both his wife and his Kapellmeister, and when the Bachs left (in two coaches with four wagon-loads of household goods) to move into the Thomasschule on May 22, his once happy and lively court must have become a sadder place. Leopold himself died in November 1728 at the age of thirty-three. The Bachs and Wilhelm Friedemann attended his interment, and Bach performed a cantata in his memory. However, until Leopold's death, he and Bach remained on good terms, and Bach and his wife sometimes revisited Cöthen and performed there. Indeed, he retained the Cöthen title of Kapellmeister *von Haus aus*, literally a non-resident Kapellmeister. As for the Prince, he remarried and in 1726 he and his second wife had a son to whom Bach dedicated a new harpsichord work, the six-movement Partita in B♭, BWV825.

Bach's signature on the title page of Cantata No. 183, Sie werden euch in den Bann tun, 1725

First Years in Leipzig

With his move to Leipzig, says Bach's biographer Jan Chiapusso, 'Bach finally was given the opportunity to enter the career to which he had pledged himself as a young man.' But a letter which he was to write some years later, on October 28, 1730, to his friend Georg Erdmann, shows that he did not take the decision easily. It is true that in it he declared, 'God ordered it that I should be called here as Director of Music and Kantor at the Thomasschule', but he went on:

Now it seemed to me at first not at all the right thing to become a Kantor after being a Kapellmeister, and I postponed my resolution for three months; but this position was described to me as so favorable that finally (especially as my sons seemed to be inclined towards study) I risked myself in the name of the Most High and came to Leipzig, took my audition {Probe} and accepted the change. And here, following God's will, I have remained until now.

As the rest of the letter shows, Bach was far from content as the Kantor to Leipzig's main churches and master at the Thomasschule. He still thought nostalgically of Cöthen, where he had enjoyed the patronage of 'a gracious prince who both loved and understood music, and with whom I had expected to end my days'. The purpose of his letter to Erdmann was to ask his friend, a diplomat serving in Danzig (now Gdańsk in Poland) if he could help him find another job. He wrote:

If Your Honor should know of or could find a suitable situation in your city for an old and faithful servant, may I humbly request you to put in a gracious recommendation for me? For

Leipzig from the south east, painted in about 1750 by Friedrich Werner

my part, I shall not fail to give satisfaction and to justify your gracious support and intercession. My present situation is worth about seven hundred thalers . . . .

It is not known what reply Erdmann made to Bach's letter. Presumably he offered no prospect of an appointment in Danzig, since Bach pursued the idea no further. However, if he was willing to consider a move to a remote Baltic port, he must have been desperate to leave Leipzig. Since he had taken up his post there, much had disappointed him:

Here, following God's will, I have remained until now. But since now, (1) I find that this post is not as remunerative as it was described to me, (2) many of the accidentia *{extra fees} of the position have been withdrawn, (3) the cost of living is very high here, and (4) the authorities are strange and little interested in music, with the result that I must live with almost constant vexation, envy and harassment, I shall be compeled, with help from the Most High, to seek my fortune elsewhere.*

Bach's reaction to the problems in Leipzig was by no means unpredictable. He had always had ideas of his own, and except at Cöthen, where he had been given freedom as far as his music was concerned, he had more often than not failed to get on with employers, who sometimes shook their heads even while recognizing his gifts. Things were much the same in Leipzig. The Thomasschule, where Bach lived and worked, had, like every institution, its jealousies, rivalries, quarrels and petty ambitions. Bach was never tactful in dealing with such matters. Nor was he willing to engage in intrigues, or take sides in minor disagreements. He was a distinguished church musician and proud of it, not a mere administrator. Yet the post which he now held called for him to be just that, along with being the director of music for the Thomaskirche and three other city churches. Jan Chiapusso has written:

Bach's superiors in Leipzig would look upon his musical performances and compositions only as one of his duties and not with respect for the musician and the sanctity of his art, as the sensitive prince in Cöthen did. Bach was clearly aware of the strong provincialism and mediocrity of the church councilors, traits which are strikingly represented by their utter failure to recognize that Bach's genius placed him far beyond the other applicants for the cantorship.

*Bach with the Thomasschule
and Thomaskirche,
the Leipzig Observatory
and his own monument,
based on a painting
by H. Bibby*

This, however, is being wise after the event. To those church councilors, Bach was no more than a senior employee, and he must have become aware of this when they interviewed him for his post. He might have been better off had he stayed at Cöthen, where, even with an unmusical princess, he would have enjoyed a civilized atmosphere and more leisure with his family, and there must have been times when he reflected bitterly that if God had summoned the princess a few months earlier, he and his wife might still be enjoying their life there. Perhaps Anna Magdalena, with her more placid temperament, told him that he had 'made his bed and must lie on it'. At least his sons could now attend the local Stadtschule, a strict institution but one with decent academic standards.

His duties as Kantor had been described only too accurately in the contract he had signed, agreeing that he would instruct the Thomasschule boys

not only in the regular classes established for that purpose, but also, without special compensation {i.e. extra fees}, in private singing lessons. I will also faithfully attend to whatever else is incumbent upon me, and furthermore, but not without the previous knowledge and consent of a noble and most wise council, in case someone should be needed to assist me in the instruction of the Latin language, will faithfully and without ado compensate the said person out of my own pocket.

It was like signing a blank check, and when things started to go wrong he may have cursed himself for putting his name to it. For example, he paid fifty thalers a year to the 'third master', Carl Friedrich Pezold, to take over the Latin teaching and some other non-musical duties, and when Pezold performed badly the council's disapproval fell on Bach. He himself instructed his choristers in the Lutheran catechism as well as musical subjects, including 'theory'.

As we have seen, his overall duties as Leipzig's director of music (in full, *Cantor zu St. Thomae et Director Musices Lipsiensis*) extended not just to the Thomaskirche but also to three other churches, and a week after taking up his post in May 1723 he had performed his Cantata No. 75 at the Nikolaikirche on May 30, Trinity Sunday. Its title was *Die Elenden sollen essen*, 'The Wretched shall Eat', and it was scored for voices, a trumpet, two oboes, oboe d'amore (an instrument pitched slightly lower than the normal oboe, with a mellower tone), strings and keyboard. Thus, immediately after his arrival, he was writing a new work, getting the parts copied and rehearsing and performing it with singers and instrumentalists whom he had only recently met.

His formal introduction to the staff and boys of the Thomasschule took place at 8:30 one morning. He knew that the choristers were the raw material whom he must use to carry out his duties in the Leipzig churches as well as in other areas of musical life controlled by the city authorities. Though he had failed to get on with his students as a young man in Arnstadt, he believed that he could manage these boys better, for he now had sons of his own and had become more flexible in his dealings with young people.

There were some fifty-five pupils at St. Thomas's, who provided the choirs for the four churches, and Bach trained the best group to sing on alternate Sundays at the Thomaskirche and Nikolaikirche. Like choirmasters today, he selected future choristers from applicants and gave individual singing lessons, and to judge from the music he wrote for them, some of these boys must have reached a high standard. He also taught keyboard playing.

Thus, Bach's Thomasschule pupils could not only sing but also play as instrumentalists. Even so, the demands of the city churches were such that he usually had to employ members of a small group of paid city musicians amounting to four wind players, four string players and an apprentice. He also employed students from Leipzig University, for whose Paulinuskirche he sometimes provided music on festive occasions. Indeed, by the second half of 1723 he had effectively become the chief musical figure of the university and in September he applied to be formally acknowledged as Director of Music and to receive the small additional salary which went with the post. When his request was turned down by the university authorities, he appealed over their heads to the Elector of Saxony in Dresden, but although he received some sympathy, he still had to accept the compromise of being responsible only for the so-called 'old services' of feast days and academic occasions, but not for the 'new' ones of regular Sunday worship, which were left to the Nikolaikirche organist, Johann Gottlieb Görner, who was already overseeing them.

It is difficult to guess why Bach so much desired this rather poorly paid appointment, which meant extra work although also giving additional prestige. As it was, this incident made him enemies, including Görner, Bach had encroached on his territory, which he justifiably resented since Bach had a more important job and hardly needed to extend it. The university was in part to blame, for they showed a preference for Bach whenever a new celebratory cantata was needed, as in December 1726 when a new professor of law was installed and Bach composed *Vereinigte Zwietracht der wechselnden Saiten*, BWV207. The same thing happened with another cantata, *Entfernet euch, ihr heitern Sterne* (now lost), written for the birthday of Elector August II of Saxony and performed before him in Leipzig's main marketplace on May 12, 1727.

The problem came to a head when the Elector's wife died in September of the same year. A university ceremony was planned and a student named Hans Carl von Kirchbach commissioned the professor of poetry, Johann Christoph Gottsched, to write the text of a tragic ode for Bach to set to music. Görner objected, claiming that he should do it, but in vain, although he was paid a small compensatory sum. This was understandable: Bach was much more talented and had already begun composing, so that even those who sympathized with Görner recognized a *fait accompli* when they saw one. Therefore, on October 17, 1727, seated at the harpsichord, Bach directed the première of his new *Trauer Ode*, addressed in flowery language to the dead Electress Christiane Eberhardine and 'written in the Italian manner', in other words operatic in style. Görner had again been slighted, but this time he was determined to defend his position and got Bach to sign an undertaking that in the future he would not enter into contracts concerning the university without proper authority.

Apart from such special occasions, the Sunday services and other church festivals, Bach also performed with his singers and instrumentalists at weddings, funerals, baptisms and civic occasions and so earned additional fees. Indeed, as his basic salary was less than a hundred thalers (much less than he had earned at Cöthen), this other work was essential. Still, he enjoyed certain benefits in kind, such as allowances for firewood, candles, corn and wine, and he and his family also lodged free in the south wing of the school. Their living quarters were cramped, but he had a big room called the *Komponirstube* or 'composition room' which was his study and office, and in which he kept the school's music library and his own.

In September 1728, Bach got into another dispute, this time with a church subdeacon who claimed his right to choose some of the music performed during Vespers (Evensong). Bach considered the choice of this music to be his business, but he lost the argument. It was hardly a serious matter, but it increased his sense of frustration. Then, in November 1730, he had to accept a reduction in the emoluments paid to him for the kind of extra work mentioned above. The Thomasschule council's reason was that he was neglecting some regular duties, including the daily singing class which he was supposed to give. Apparently he gave no satisfactory explanation; instead he sent them a memorandum demanding better facilities. In particular, he stated that to perform church cantatas adequately required at least a dozen competent singers plus about eighteen instrumentalists including oboes, bassoons, trumpets, timpani and a dozen string players, adding that a couple of flautists were also desirable. However, he complained, there was a general shortage of instrumentalists: he usually had only around eight and so had to seek out others from the university who had to be paid for their trouble, or use choristers whom he needed for singing. He then went on to say that only seventeen of his fifty-four Thomasschule pupils were really good enough to perform in public; as for the rest, twenty needed more training and the rest were plain incompetent. Needless to say, this was not what the council wished to hear, and his demands were ignored.

Leaving aside musical matters, the Thomasschule could not have been much of a home for Bach and his growing family, and it is certain that he never enjoyed the part of his duties that required him to be a schoolmaster and disciplinarian. The school rules stated that

As soon as the bell rings (at five o'clock in summer, six in winter), each pupil must rise, wash and comb himself, and be ready in a quarter of an hour to come down for prayers bring his Bible. Clothes, shoes, stockings and linen must be kept clean . . . Before bedtime, the day's lessons must be recited and the Most High thanked for what has been learned . . . Before and after midday and evening meals, the boy whose turn it is will say grace and the others will repeat it after him. During the meal shall be read aloud a Psalm or a chapter from the Bible or some other edifying book.

A view of Leipzig University in 1798, as seen from the Neumarkt

As for the building itself, it dated from 1553 and was drafty and uncomfortable. The boys (called *Alumnen*) were mostly from poor homes and not always in robust health or well clothed, yet besides their strict school regime and church duties they had to sing out of doors on feast days, some of which, such as Epiphany in early January, could be bitterly cold. Similarly, a Sunday service in the Thomaskirche or Nikolaikirche normally began at seven in the morning and lasted three hours. Colds (and worse illnesses) must have been endemic among the choristers and spread quickly in their cramped quarters, where they often had to share beds. Even by the standards of the time, people knew that these living conditions were inadequate, and a report of 1728 reads:

> *Thirst was unbearable, especially in the hot days of summer. Further, it afflicted many poor children who, having no means of support from home, often had to climb over the water urn that stood in the chamber and drink in common with the rats, which at that time were present in frightful numbers.*

The poor boys had to endure much. And not only the boys. The Bachs' quarters were separated from theirs only by a thin wall, and although they knew of the choristers' discomfort they could do nothing to relieve it. As for the Rektor (headmaster), he was an aged man who had been there for four long decades and probably resisted change. Though Bach himself had been to a strict boarding school and could do without creature comforts, he must have felt that this was a poor home for his wife and family. Anna Magdalena bore him no fewer than thirteen children in this depressing place, of whom seven died in infancy.

The Thomasschule, Leipzig

Frustrations and Achievements

B ach remained in his Leipzig post and was to die in the city twenty-seven years after his arrival there. Little by little, it must have become clearer to him that he would never escape to a better position, and at times he may have felt great bitterness. Yet as a deeply religious man, he seems also to have accepted that this was what God meant for him.

Despite, or perhaps because of, his unhappiness, Bach wrote music during the Leipzig years that is dazzling both in quality and sheer quantity. It has been calculated that if a professional music copyist were to set about writing the notes of all Bach's musical scores, working a thirty-five-hour week, it would take him a lifetime; Bach, of course, composed the music as well as writing and performing it. During his first ten years there, he undertook the enormous task of composing cantatas to correspond with the events of the church year, which amounted to around sixty in each year. The initial motive for this was the requirement for a cantata and a motet (a shorter vocal piece) to be performed during the long Sunday services at the Thomaskirche and Nikolaikirche, the cantata following the Gospel and preceding the Creed, and it seems to have been expected of the Kantor that these should be specially written rather than drawn from existing music in his library.

The organ of the Thomaskirche in Leipzig

One of Bach's musicians, the trumpeter Gottfried Reiche (1667–1734), painted by E. G. Hausmann

Accordingly, Bach composed a cantata every week, producing something like twenty minutes of music for voices and instruments, which then had to be copied (the individual parts for around sixteen singers and eighteen instrumentalists) and rehearsed. The texts, all with biblical themes, were also specially written. Bach used several librettists, but his favorite became a man called Picander, the pen name for Christian Friedrich Henrici (1700–64), a local civil servant who composed about 300 church cantatas at Leipzig. By 1725, Bach had written, rehearsed and performed two complete cycles of cantatas; a third followed by 1727, and a fourth by 1729 – that is, 240 substantial pieces of music in six years. By the 1740s, a fifth cycle existed. Unfortunately, around a hundred of these works have been lost, mostly the later ones, which is all the more a pity since Bach was never content simply to repeat himself and these later pieces may have had beauties that we cannot imagine.

Unbelievably, Bach also produced other church works that are towering masterpieces. There is his setting of the Magnificat (originally in the key of E♭) that he first performed on Christmas Day 1723 and later revised as the Magnificat in D, BWV243, that we know today. The Christmas Oratorio, BWV248, which is really a sequence of six cantatas partly adapted from earlier music, dates in its final form from the Christmas and New Year of 1734–5, when the various sections were given in turn. Similarly, the great Mass in B minor, BWV232, is actually made up of several pieces that he wrote independently from 1723 onwards, and finally assembled much later. He used the Kyrie and Gloria in 1733 as part of a petition to the Elector of Saxony for a court title, but the whole work as we know it today, with its five main sections (Kyrie, Gloria, Credo, Sanctus and Agnus Dei) further divided into twenty-four separate numbers, probably dates from 1749, when Bach was nearing the end of his life.

Music such as this, created under difficult conditions by a man discontented with his job, is quite extraordinary and some people react to it with the kind of wonder that expresses itself in flowery language. Thus the German scholar Fritz Volbach wrote:

The Bach B minor Mass soars above us like some huge, primitive mountain rock. Its summit is lost in the clouds in an infinity of sunlit blue, lonely and sublime, it is unapproachable by any other music. The art of Bach is one which yearns towards the eternal; through love and the grace of God it finds the way, love which entwines the transient with the everlasting, the finite with the infinite. This is a longing towards the unknown, all that is unrevealed, a longing only to be stilled by yearning . . . Who more fitted to depict the glory of this vast heavenly kingdom, to tread this secret land of longing lying far beyond the world of reality, than J. S. Bach, the greatest German mystic?

Fine words, but the music itself is finer. With its grandeur and gentleness, the B minor Mass stands as a monument of Christian sacred music, its moods ranging from the choral supplication of the opening Kyrie (in a subdued B minor) to the tremendous D major outburst of praise that is the Sanctus. No sympathetic hearer to the Credo will easily forget the drooping phrases and piercing E minor harmonies of the choral number over a throbbing bass that sets the words 'Crucifixus etiam pro nobis sub Pontio Pilato, passus et sepultus est', nor the great shout of D major joy which then follows with the words 'Et resurrexit'.

'One must either believe or suspend disbelief': this was the advice given by the British tenor Sir Peter Pears in 1986 to pupils studying the solo vocal roles in Bach's *St. Matthew Passion*, BWV244. This other masterpiece of the Leipzig years was first performed on Good Friday, April 11, 1727. Compared to the B minor Mass, it is more human and consciously dramatic, with Picander's text being not in Latin but in the

*A page of the
autograph score
of the St. Matthew Passion*

German that the Leipzig congregation could understand. It tells the story of Christ's passion, beginning with the decision of the priests to arrest him and going right through to his burial. Here there are no less than seventy-eight separate musical sections, which may be long or short, solo or choral; here, too, are operatic forms such as recitative and aria as well as traditional Lutheran chorales, sometimes set with striking harmony. As for the choruses, they can represent either a faithful Christian congregation, in such solemn hymns as 'O Sacred Head sore Wounded', or the Jerusalem crowd who yell 'Barabbas' or 'Let him be crucified!' There is no comforting resurrection message in this work intended to be heard only on Good Friday, one of the most solemn days of the Christian year. Instead it ends with a sad chorus in a minor key which is a kind of sublime saraband, for Bach knew how to use dance styles in sacred music, just as Luther had taken folk tunes and turned them into uplifting hymns.

There is an extraordinary intensity about the music of the *St. Matthew Passion*. One famous scene is that in which the disciple Peter, having been told by Jesus that he will deny him before cockcrow, does indeed do so, angrily. The Evangelist (a narrator's role given to a tenor voice) then tells us that Peter remembers Christ's words, and 'went out, and wept bitterly'. These words are sung to a long, sighing phrase which is like a howl of despair. Indeed, although Bach never composed an opera, here is a work which is operatic in almost every respect. Its 'Christus' is a real role, sung by a baritone who is accompanied by the rich sound (which has been likened to a halo) of

A performance of one of Bach's Passions that took place two hundred years after his birth on 16 May 1885. Among the performers is a bust of the composer

a string orchestra rather than the drier one of the harpsichord used for the Evangelist's narrative telling the story in the words of St. Matthew's Gospel.

Even this great work does not stand alone, for Bach's *St. John Passion*, BWV245, was composed three years earlier and first performed on Good Friday, April 7, 1724. Here, too, is powerful and profound music. Bach's biographer Malcolm Boyd says of both works that they unfold 'on four interlocking levels: the narrative (or dramatic), the lyrical, the devotional and the monumental'.

It is not surprising that between 1723 and 1729, Bach's new works were almost entirely restricted to church music. However, there are a few organ and harpsichord pieces, the former perhaps composed when he inspected new or rebuilt organs, inaugurated new ones – for example, when he went forty miles to Gera in June 1724 to play new organs in two churches, receiving a fee of thirty thalers and expenses – or simply gave recitals, as he did at the Sophienkirche in Dresden in September 1725.

Early in 1729, and apparently at his own request, Bach took over the direction of Leipzig University's *collegium musicum*, or music society. It seems that he wanted to have another area besides church music in which to work and that he found the enthusiastic, music-loving students worthy material. They performed in an outdoor coffee-garden in the summer and in Zimmermann's Coffeehouse in the winter, singing and playing all kinds of music, including Bach's. He probably performed with them some of the music that he had written at Cöthen, and composed for them two of his orchestral suites, including No. 2 in B minor with its prominent flute part. (This was clearly written for a gifted young player, who perhaps also played his Flute Sonata in the same key, BWV1030.) The secular cantata *Phoebus and Pan* and the 'Coffee' Cantata (*Schweigt stille, plaudert nicht*, BWV211, also with a flute part) are genial, easy-going and above all witty pieces. The first is based on a comic tale by Ovid and the second tells of a girl whose secret but innocent passion is drinking coffee, which must have pleased Gottfried Zimmermann and his clients. Another jolly piece is the 'Peasant' Cantata of 1742 (*Mer hahn en neue Oberkeet*), a bucolic affair using local dialect instead of formal High German and with a part for a rural-sounding horn. All three of these pieces had words by Picander, who may have found it a relief not to have to produce yet another pious church text. Bach, too, must have enjoyed this new area of his activities which allowed him to write lighter music. Although he gave up full-time direction of the *collegium musicum* in 1737, when his pupil Carl Gotthelf Gerlach took over, he kept up strong links with it.

By 1731, Bach had completed the Six Partitas, BWV825–30, which formed the first part of the *Clavier-Übung*, and which he himself published. In 1735 he wrote his Concerto in the Italian Style, BWV971, a vigorous three-movement work intended for a two-manual harpsichord. Soon after this, he started to work seriously on the second book of his monumental set of forty-eight preludes and fugues, *Das Wohltemperirte Clavier*, BWV870-93, but only completed it in 1742. The title, meaning 'The Well-tempered Keyboard', refers not to good humor but to the 'equal temperament' tuning system, then fairly new, which made semitone steps on keyboard instruments equidistant and allowed any note to be a keynote. (Without this system, some keys were more 'in tune' than others.) As in the first book, here were twenty-four preludes and fugues proceeding through all the available major and minor keys. Despite the seemingly abstract nature of this enterprise, they cover a wide range of moods and show Bach's complete mastery of his craft.

In June 1730, the Thomasschule acquired a new Rektor following the death of the elderly incumbent. Johann Matthias Gesner at once set about an extensive rebuilding program that improved the pupils' quarters and those of the staff. Bach must have been relieved, for his family was now numerous; in this year he proudly said that he and they could already form an ensemble of singers and players. For some months they moved out into temporary accommodation in the Hainstrasse. On reoccupying the new buildings in June 1732, Bach composed a celebratory cantata, *Froher Tag, verlangte Stunden*, 'Happy Day, Desired Hour'.

Middle Years in Leipzig

With Gesner's installation as Rektor in 1730, the Thomasschule became a more congenial place for Bach and his family. The new headmaster genuinely appreciated Bach's musicianship and liked him as a man, and some years later he was to write admiringly of him at the organ, 'running over the keys of the instrument of instruments, whose innumerable pipes are brought to life by bellows, with both hands and, with the utmost speed, with his feet, producing by himself the most various and at the same time mutually agreeable combinations of sounds in orderly procession.' Gesner was no less impressed by the way his Kantor rehearsed his singers and players, noting that he missed nothing in the way of correctness of notes and time and liked to sing out cues to his singers. Here, he wrote, was 'this one man taking in all these harmonies with his keen ear and emitting with his voice alone the tone of all the voices. Favorer as I am of antiquity, the accomplishments of our Bach, and of any other that there may be like him, appear to me to effect what not many Orpheuses, nor twenty Arions, could achieve.'

Soon after his arrival at the Thomasschule, Gesner helped Bach by reminding his colleagues that this was not just a school but 'a seminary of music whereby the singing in all our churches might be provided'. He also obtained for him the restoration of the extra fees *(Accidentien)*, which had recently been reduced by a church council puzzled by and somewhat dissatisfied with their prickly Kantor. But unfortunately for Bach and his family, this gifted and ambitious man was to remain in Leipzig for only four years before he accepted a new and better post at Göttingen University.

The man who succeeded him in 1734 was much younger, and only three years older than Bach's oldest son Wilhelm Friedemann. He was Johann August Ernesti, a fine scholar aged twenty-seven who was already teaching at the Thomasschule. He and his Kantor, now nearly fifty, seem to have started on good terms and Ernesti was godfather to the Bachs' last two sons, Johann August Abraham (born in 1733) and Johann Christian (born in 1735). But before long he made clear his progressive, 'Enlightenment' views as to the Thomasschule's role in serving the church, which included the belief that music's place in worship should be that of a mere adjunct. Indeed, he treated it with some contempt, coming across a pupil practicing the violin and enquiring if he, too, 'wanted to be an inn fiddler'.

Ernesti's firm priority for the Thomasschule was academic excellence, and he and his Kantor were soon at odds over the considerable demands that Bach placed on pupils' time for rehearsals, music copying and the like. Then came a major clash in August 1736 over their respective spheres of authority. When Bach's choir prefect punished some younger choristers for misbehaving during a wedding service, one of them complained to Ernesti, who not only condemned the punishment but also, despite Bach's pleading, ordered the prefect to be flogged in the presence of the school. Rather than accept this indignity, the prefect, who was about to go to university, left the school altogether, whereupon Ernesti, without consulting Bach, appointed a replacement choir prefect whom Bach considered to be musically inadequate and of poor character.

Bach now complained bitterly in a series of letters addressed first to the Thomasschule council, then to the Dresden church consistory, and finally to the Elector himself. His first letter, dated August 12, begged the council to inform Ernesti that, according to the normal practice of the school, 'the Kantor should select choir prefects for musical competence without interference on the Rektor's part'. On the same day, a

Sunday, he went to his choir loft for a service, saw the unwanted new prefect (Johann Gottlob Krause) in charge and dismissed him. But by the time of a second service later that day, Ernesti had reinstated him and on discovering this Bach drove Krause from the choir loft with 'loud cries and noise' that were heard by the waiting congregation. The next day he wrote again to the council, accusing the Rektor of undermining his authority, and two days later he sent them yet another letter explaining his objections to Krause. Ernesti then put his own case in writing, claiming among other things, that his Kantor 'should fulfill his office with greater diligence', which seems preposterous given his proven energy and capacity for work.

Bach had demanded that Ernesti be reprimanded, but the Thomasschule council did not want to offend their Rektor, who now made further criticisms of Bach's integrity and even veracity. Matters dragged on in what must have been a poisonous atmosphere until, on receiving a Dresden court title in November, Bach asked the consistory there to protect his position and instruct the Rektor accordingly. He even wrote to the Elector, asking him 'to direct the council not to molest my prerogative of appointing the *praefecto chori musici*' and 'graciously to order the consistory here to demand an apology from Rektor Ernesti for the indignity put upon me'. The Elector took Bach seriously and ordered the consistory to look into the matter with the Thomasschule council. Eventually it was decided that Ernesti should be admonished for his dealings with Bach, but that Bach, too, should be reprimanded for allowing prefects to undertake duties that he himself should have carried out, such as directing the choir at weddings. As for the wretched Krause, he was told to remain as choir prefect until he left the Thomasschule a few months later.

Bach with his sons (from left to right)
Johann Gottfried Bernhard, Carl Philipp Emanuel and Wilhelm Friedrich, painted in 1730 by Balthasar Denner

To the Elector of Saxony, this must have seemed a very small matter. However, he may have been genuinely sympathetic to Bach's cause, and perhaps proved it when he attended Leipzig's Easter Fair on April 28, 1738 and Bach and his *collegium musicum* performed for him. The new work was a festive secular cantata called *Willkommen! Ihr herrschenden Götter*, and offered fulsome praise of this earthly ruler with the words 'Welcome, ye reigning gods of the earth'.

Thus Bach in his early middle age was, as ever, a man of strong principle, pugnacious and inflexible in defending his position. Neither he nor his Rektor did their reputations any good by their public quarrel, but after the dust of battle had settled somehow things went on much as before, and the combatants, doubtless weary of conflict, seem to have accepted that they could continue to work together.

It was during these troubled years that Bach's oldest sons grew up. Wilhelm Friedemann was twenty in 1730 and completed his university studies three years later, going on to become the part-time organist of the Sophienkirche in Dresden. Carl Philipp Emanuel, three-and-a-half years younger, left Leipzig in 1734, when he entered the University of Frankfurt in the city of Frankfurt an der Oder. As for Johann Gottfried Bernhard, born in May 1715, when he was twenty his father managed to secure for him the position of organist at the Marienkirche in Mühlhausen, a church which had heard Bach's own music nearly three decades earlier.

Although these three sons were musically gifted, they did not automatically assume they would follow in their father's footsteps. Carl Philipp Emanuel, although he had been his father's pupil and assistant and already had several compositions to his credit by 1734, went to Frankfurt to study law rather than music. This does not necessarily mean that he planned to practice as a lawyer, or that his father forced this on him: it has rightly been said that 'his actions seem to indicate that he simply wanted to keep

Frederick the Great
of Prussia
as Crown Prince,
painted in 1745
by Antoine Pesne

his options open as long as possible, and that he was guided and encouraged in that by Sebastian'. It seems certain, however, that Bach wanted his sons to have the university education that he himself had missed, knowing that it would give them the professional status without which an individual might be treated as slightingly as he had sometimes been during his own career. In the event, Carl Philipp Emanuel did become a musician, serving in the court of King Frederick the Great of Prussia for nearly three decades from 1738–67. At the same time, he was also at home in the company of literary people and intellectuals, and acquired a lawyer-like precision in his management of money. In 1755, five years after his father's death, he applied for his Leipzig post but was unsuccessful. Eventually he succeeded Telemann as Kantor to the principal churches of Hamburg on the death of the older man, who, as his godfather, probably recommended.

Wilhelm Friedemann Bach's position as an organist in Dresden, dating from 1733, came about through his father's strengthening links with that city. Bach took his *collegium musicum* of university students to Dresden from time to time, and played the fine Sophienkirche organ by Gottfried Silbermann before his son started working there. It was at this time, too, that he became friendly with the opera composer Johann Adolf Hasse (1699–1783) and, since he traveled to Dresden in September 1731 to give organ recitals in the city's churches and at court, he probably attended the première of Hasse's opera *Cleofide*, which took place at court on the thirteenth of that month. An early writer on Bach, Johann Nikolaus Forkel, told the story of how Bach liked to go with 'Friede' (perhaps his favorite child) to see operas and 'hear the pretty songs', and although the remark has been taken to imply condescension, it is more likely that he simply enjoyed this music. It was also in these years that he sent the Kyrie and Gloria of his Mass in B minor to the new Elector of Saxony, August III, with the request for a court title, mentioning the 'undeserved affronts' that he suffered in Leipzig and from which he thought a court appointment might protect him. At the time, he was unsuccessful, but on November 19, 1736 he gained the title of *Hofcompositeur* (court composer) to the Saxon court. It is understandable that he wished to see his sons rise above the pettiness of a church Kantor's life under unimaginative authorities.

Unfortunately, Friedemann did not fulfill all his early promise and had a disappointing life, although he was known as a superb organist. In 1746 he was appointed to the Liebfrauenkirche in Halle. However, things did not work out well there for Friedmann, partly because of his free-thinking turn of mind and partly because he often went in search of other posts, thus demonstrating his dissatisfaction with the one that he held. After demanding a rise in pay in 1761, receiving a curt refusal, and finally leaving his job without notice in 1764, he embarked on what was to be twenty years as a freelance teacher, organist and composer. He died in poverty, and before doing so he was reduced to selling off some of his father's manuscripts and putting J. S. Bach's name to some of his own compositions.

Though Bach did not live to see his beloved Friede's decline, he had early problems with his third son, Johann Gottfried Bernhard Bach. Soon after this young man of twenty took up his Mühlhausen post in 1735, he fell into debt. Bach then helped him to obtain the post (perhaps better paid) of organist at the Jakobikirche in Sangerhausen, the very one that he himself had failed to obtain as a young man because of the intervention of the reigning duke in favor of another candidate; Divine Providence, he told the church council, now allowed them to give the post to a Bach, just as they had intended then. But by May 1738, Johann Bernhard was again in financial trouble and fled the town leaving unpaid bills. The mayor wrote to Bach, whom he knew, to tell him what had happened, and Bach replied in distress and embarrassment:

I have not set eyes on my unfortunately wayward son since last year . . . Now I learn with the deepest dismay that he has again contracted various debts, has not in the least mended his ways, but has absconded without giving me the smallest indication of where he is staying. What more can I say or do? Since no admonition, not even loving provision and assistance, will suffice any longer, I must patiently bear my cross and simply leave my undutiful son to God's mercy, not doubting that He will hear my sorrowful prayers and finally, according to his Holy Will, bring him to know that conversion comes only from Holy Virtue. Since I have now opened my heart to Your Honor, I am fully confident that you will not impute to me the bad conduct of my son, but will recognize that a devoted father whose children are dear to him will do all he can to help promote their well-being. It was this that made me recommend my son, when you had the vacancy . . . I beg Your Honor to kindly make enquiries as to his where-abouts, and then you need only give me definite information so that a final effort may be made to see if, with God's help, his obduracy can be won over and he can be made to see his errors.

In fact, Johann Gottfried Bernhard had gone fifty miles south to Jena, where he matriculated at the University in January 1739 and intended, like Carl Philipp Emanuel, to study law. But soon after, news reached Leipzig that deeply grieved his father: he had contracted an infection and died on May 27.

The Last Years

Despite the departure of three sons, Bach's household must have been crowded at this time. When Johann Gottfried left for Mühlhausen in 1735, four children remained whose ages ranged between three and twenty-six, and three more were to be born between that year and 1742. In October 1737, his nephew Johann Elias Bach (1705–55) joined the household as a secretary and tutor to the children; he was soon sending home to his mother for flowers for Anna Magdalena's garden and to a friend for a tame linnet whose singing might give her pleasure. For a gift to his uncle, he knew that wine was always acceptable and he was happy to offer it, and it was perhaps he who helped bring to the house other musicians such as the lutenist Silvius Weiss, for whom Bach may have composed his Partita in C minor, BWV997.

Portrait of J. S. Bach in pastel by Gottlieb Friedrich Bach (1714–85)

Even so, these were difficult years for the great musician, and it has been suggested by his biographer Hannsdieter Wohlfarth that he felt an 'increasing inner isolation'. Wohlfarth suggests that 'after about 1735 he began to become aware of his historical mission and to understand this mission as imposing tasks he still had to fulfill'. Thus he completed and published keyboard works (for harpsichord, or clavichord, rather than organ) in a series that he called *Clavier–Übung*, literally 'keyboard exercise'. The first volume had dated from 1731 and included the Six Partitas, while this second one had another Partita in B minor, labeled 'in the French style', and the *Concerto nach italiänischen Gusto*, nowadays usually called the *Italian Concerto* (the word *gusto* means 'taste'). The remaining two volumes of this series, published 1739–42, were to contain organ works such as the 'St. Anne' Prelude and Fugue in E♭, BWV552, and the Goldberg Variations, BWV988, a monumental set of thirty variations for harpsichord on a stately theme that Bach had written several years before.

An often told story of this latter piece is that Bach was commissioned to write it by the Russian ambassador to Saxony, Count Keyserlingk, who suffered from insomnia and wanted music that his young harpsichordist Johann Gottlieb Goldberg (a Bach pupil) could play to him at night to help him sleep. But as Goldberg was only about fourteen and the music (written for a two-manual harpsichord) extremely difficult, it seems unlikely, although Forkel claimed that Bach received for it a golden goblet containing a hundred louis d'or. Another possibility is that the music is so inventive and challenging that it was intended instead to while away the count's waking hours and, at the same time, give his young harpsichordist plenty to do. Whatever the case, Bach gave the count a copy.

Although he now enjoyed some fame, Bach also met controversy, and perhaps for the first time found his achievements questioned. In May 1737 a fellow musician, Johann Adolf Scheibe, published an article which praised his compositional mastery and his artistry as a performer but declared of his works that 'his bombastic and intricate procedures deprived them of naturalness and obscured their beauty by an excess of art'.

*The title page
from a 1794 edition
of one of Bach's
keyboard concertos,
showing eight musicians*

One knows what he meant: there is an ornate quality in Bach's work and sometimes an intellectual rigor that may be thought forbidding. Judged by anyone whose musical aim is simplicity and directness, Bach may be judged to fall short. Yet it has rightly been said that the problem simply 'lies in a clash of irreconcilable stylistic ideals'; other composers offer different kinds of music, but Bach had to remain himself and we should judge him in those terms. A reasoned reply to Scheibe's article was prepared by a Leipzig University lecturer called Johann Abraham Birnbaum and appeared in January 1738; Bach himself may have had a hand in it, since he distributed copies to friends.

By now, he seems to have resigned himself to staying in his Leipzig post but to have become weary of it, and someone's suggestion, in 1739, that permission might be obtained for another performance of the *St. Matthew Passion* elicited from him the cool response that it had already been performed and another performance would only burden him. He might remain in his thankless position, but from now on he was, as far as possible, working for himself.

He still traveled from time to time, inspecting church organs and giving recitals. In August 1741 he went to Berlin to see his son Carl Philipp Emanuel at Frederick the Great's Potsdam court, and within a few weeks of his return he was off again, visiting Count Keyserlingk in Dresden. At home, he taught a number of gifted, carefully chosen pupils, amongst whom was Johann Christoph Altnikol (1719–59), a Leipzig University student who later married Bach's daughter Elizabeth Juliana Friederika, born in 1726. His jolly 'Peasant' Cantata was performed on August 30,1742 at an estate near Leipzig called Kleinzschocher, in cheerful homage to its new owner, Carl Heinrich von Dieskau. There were now very few new sacred cantatas, although Nos. 197 (written for a wedding) and 200 are among them. He had lost interest in such

Frederick the Great in 1745,
by Antoine Pesne

music, it seems, and was content to perform older pieces, although part of the Credo in his B minor Mass dates from the 1740s. In around 1745 he also began looking through some of his earlier organ pieces from the Weimar years, revising them and making a collection, BWV651–68, as well as arranging six more from movements in his church cantatas, the so-called 'Schübler' Chorales, BWV645–50.

During the 1740s, Bach also took an enthusiastic and approving interest in the pianos being made by the organ builder Gottfried Silbermann. The pianoforte was then a new instrument and differed from the harpsichord in that its strings were struck instead of being plucked and so could play 'soft and loud', hence the name. He was to play more pianos in 1747 during the most important and best documented visit of these years, when he made his second visit to Potsdam in May of that year, probably at the invitation of King Frederick the Great himself.

He had several reasons for going. One was that his son Carl had married and he already had a grandson of eighteen months whom he wished to see; it had not been possible to go earlier because of the political differences between Prussia and Saxony. He traveled with 'Friede', who also wished to see his brother, and their encounter with the king came immediately after their arrival on Sunday, May 7, as a contemporary newspaper account reports:

In the evening, at about the time when the usual chamber music began in the royal apartments, His Majesty was informed that Kapellmeister Bach had arrived in Potsdam and that he was at that very moment in the king's antechamber awaiting His Majesty's permission to listen to the music. The king immediately ordered that he should be allowed to enter, and as he did so His Majesty went to the so-called forte-and-piano and condescended, in person and without any preparation, to play to Kapellmeister Bach a theme on which to improvise a fugue. This the Kapellmeister did so successfully that not only was His Majesty moved to express his most gracious satisfaction with it, but all those present were astonished. Herr Bach found the theme he was given of such unusual beauty that he intends to work it out on paper as a regular fugue and have it engraved on copper. On Monday this famous man played on the organ of the Church of the Holy Ghost in Potsdam, earning universal applause from the many who heard him. In the evening His Majesty once again commanded him to execute a fugue in six parts, which he did with the same skill as on the previous occasion, to the king's satisfaction and the admiration of all.

Some years later, Wilhelm Friedemann Bach also gave an account of these events which reminds us that Frederick the Great was a bright amateur flautist. It differs somewhat from the above account, but complements it and probably reflects events more accurately. He told Bach's biographer Forkel:

At this time, the king had a private concert every evening at which he generally performed some concertos on the flute. One evening, just as he was getting his flute ready and his musicians were assembled, an officer brought with him a list of the strangers who had arrived. With his flute in his hand, he ran over the list and immediately turned to the assembled musicians and said with a kind of agitation, 'Gentlemen, old Bach has come.' The flute was now laid aside and old Bach, who had alighted at his son's lodgings, was immediately summoned to the palace.

The king gave up the evening's concert and invited Bach, then already called 'the old Bach', to try his fortepianos made by Silbermann, which stood in several rooms of the palace. The musicians went with him from room to room, and Bach was invited everywhere to try them and play unpremeditated compositions {improvisations}. After he had done so for some time, he asked the king to give him a theme for a fugue, in order to execute it immediately and without any preparation. The king admired the learned manner in which his theme was treated extempore and, probably to see how far such art could be carried, expressed a wish to hear a fugue with six obligato parts. But as not every subject is suited to such full harmony, Bach chose one himself and immediately executed it to the astonishment of all in the same magnificent and learned manner as he had done for that of the king.

His Majesty also desired to hear his organ playing. So the next day Bach was taken to all the organs in Potsdam, as he had before been taken to Silbermann's fortepianos. After his return to Leipzig, he composed the theme which he had received from the king in three and six parts, added several composed passages in strict canon to it, had it engraved {printed} under the title 'Musical Offering' and dedicated it to its inventor.

Thus Bach, now sixty-two and nearing the end of his life, saw his genius appreciated in a way that had never seemed possible in Leipzig. His composition of the *Musikalisches Opfer*, BWV1079, which was published later in the same year and dedicated to the king, seems to acknowledge this, for in this multi-sectioned work with the royal theme at its center he displayed his enormous command of the art to which he had dedicated his life. Some of its sections represent the noblest imaginable achievements of polyphony, although others are lighter and offer a rococo charm, with the flute (the king's instrument) often leading the proceedings.

On returning to Leipzig, Bach joined a 'Society for the Musical Sciences' founded by his former pupil Lorenz Christoph Mizler, and sent its members some intricate examples of his polyphonic art. However, according to C. P. E. Bach, he had no time for the 'dry, mathematical matters' that Mizler and his friends sometimes wanted to discuss; instead, he is supposed to have said that 'music should move the heart with sweet emotion', and never considered himself a mere intellectual.

Between 1745 and 1750, he also composed other polyphonic pieces, which are crowned by another monumental work whose very title, *The Art of Fugue*, suggests that he was making a conscious bequest to posterity and in so doing summing up his

A musical performance on the flute by Frederick the Great in a nineteenth century painting

art as a composer. Having completed it, he then started work on a revision, which breaks off after some two hundred bars of a majestic fugue with four subjects, one of which is based on his own name in the German nomenclature for musical notes. (The notes are B♭, A, C and B♭ natural.) C. P. E. Bach was later to write, 'Over this fugue, in which the name Bach is used as a countersubject, its creator died.'

In his last years, Bach suffered increasingly from eye trouble: cataract affected both eyes and eventually he became completely blind. By 1749 he was no longer able to carry out his Kantor's duties, and the last examples of his handwriting are very irregular. In June of that year the Thomasschule council, never tactful, invited Johann Gottlob Harrer to audition for the post of Kantor 'in case the Kapellmeister and Kantor Herr Sebast. Bach should die'.

In October, the now elderly and ailing musician was to have been a godfather at the birth of his Altnikol grandson, named Johann Sebastian after him, but he was unable to do so. Ever a fighter, in March 1750 he invited the English oculist John Taylor to treat his condition. However, although at first his sight improved, it quickly deteriorated again and a second unsuccessful operation left him weakened and depressed. None-the-less, in May he accepted into his house a new pupil, Johann Gottfried Müthel, and in July, amazingly, his sight briefly returned. On July 22, he took what was to be his last Holy Communion, in his own home, and died six days later of a stroke.

Bach left an estate consisting of bonds and cash, manuscripts and many musical instruments, in all valued at some 1,100 thalers. But it had to be divided between his widow and his nine surviving children, and Anna Magdalena, to whom the Thomasschule council granted just six months' pension, lived for ten years in relative poverty with her unmarried step-daughter and two younger daughters. No Thomasschule choristers sang at her funeral in 1760, but she was buried beside her husband.

Bach at the Potsdam court of Frederick the Great in 1747, playing the organ for the King

Carl Philipp Emanuel Bach should perhaps have done more to help his widowed stepmother; living in Potsdam, he may have known little of her circumstances, but seems not to have made enquiries. As for Wilhelm Friedemann, his career was already troubled and perhaps he had little spare cash to send to a stepmother. Among Anna Magdalena's own sons who later distinguished themselves as musicians, Johann Christian Bach (1735–82) inherited three of his father's harpsichords and quickly left Leipzig to go first to his brother at Potsdam and then on to Italy, where he pursued his musical studies and acquired a noble patron. He became a Catholic and an organist of Milan Cathedral, but soon found his *métier* as a composer of Italian operas. By 1762, he had received operatic offers from London, and he then made his home in the English capital, striking up a friendship there with the boy Mozart in 1764. We do not know if he ever helped his mother financially.

It was through J. C. Bach that Mozart became aware of J. S. Bach's importance. Beethoven also knew of him and once called him 'the immortal god of harmony'; the powerful fugues in his later quartets and sonatas owe much to the earlier master. But the general public had long forgotten his name when another German composer, Mendelssohn, showed, by his revival of the *St. Matthew Passion* in Berlin in March 1829, that Bach's work had qualities which made it of permanent relevance to anyone who cared about music. Today this German court and church musician is universally recognized as a giant even among the great composers and is perhaps, to quote Wagner, 'the most stupendous miracle in all music'.

The Bach monument in Leipzig, created in 1908 by Carl Soffner

j.s.bach

the complete works

Bach did not number his works. They were catalogued in a thematic index by Wolfgang Schmider in 1950 and the numbers are preceded by the initials BWV, *Bach Werke-Vereichnis,* which means Index to Bach's Works. Bach's church cantatas are listed here by their BWV numbers, however, they can also be referred to by number without the BWV prefix. Some of the works ascribed to Bach in the Index are now thought to be of doubtful authorship and they are not included in the following list. Dates are given where known.

BWV1	Cantata, Wie schön leuchtet der Morgenstern, chorale (1725)
BWV2	Cantata, Ach Gott, vom Himmel sieh darein, chorale, (1724)
BWV3	Cantata, Ach Gott, wie manches, Herzeleid, chorale (1725)
BWV4	Cantata, Christ lag in Todes Banden, chorale (?1707–8)
BWV5	Cantata, Wo soll ich fliehen hin, chorale (1724)
BWV6	Cantata, Bleib bei uns, denn es will Abend werden (1725)
BWV7	Cantata, Christ unser Herr zum Jordan kam, chorale (1724)
BWV8	Cantata, Liebster Gott, wann werd ich sterben?, chorale (1724)
BWV9	Cantata, Es ist das Heil uns kommen her, chorale (c.1732–5)
BWV10	Cantata, Meine Seel erhebt den Herren (1724)
BWV11	Cantata, Lobet Gott in seinen Reichen, Ascension Oratorio (1735)
BWV12	Cantata, Weinen, Klagen, Sorgen, Zagen (1714)
BWV13	Cantata, Meine Seufzer, meine Tränen (1726)
BWV14	Cantata, Wär Gott nicht mit uns diese Zeit, chorale (1735)
BWV16	Cantata, Herr Gott, dich loben wir (1726)
BWV17	Cantata, Wer Dank opfert, der preiset mich (1726)

Cantata, Gleichwie der Regen und   **BWV18**
Schnee vom Himmel fällt (c.1714)

Cantata, Es erhub sich ein Streit (1726)   **BWV19**

Cantata, O Ewigkeit, du Donnerwort, chorale (1724)   **BWV20**

Cantata, Ich hatte viel Bekümmernis (?1714)   **BWV21**

Cantata, Jesus nahm zu sich die Zwölfe (1723)   **BWV22**

Cantata, Du wahrer Gott und Davids Sohn (1723)   **BWV23**

Cantata, Ein ungefärbt Gemüte (1723)   **BWV24**

Cantata, Es ist nicht Gesundes an meinem Leibe (1723)   **BWV25**

Cantata, Ach wie nichtig, ach wie nichtig, chorale (1724)   **BWV26**

Cantata, Wer weiss, wie nahe mir mein Ende!, chorale (1726)   **BWV27**

Cantata, Gottlob! nun geht das Jahr zu Ende (1725)   **BWV28**

Cantata, Wir danken dir, Gott, wir danken dir (1731)   **BWV29**

Cantata, Freue dich, erlöste Schar (c.1738)   **BWV30**

Cantata, Angenehmes Widerau, freue dich (1737)   **BWV30***a*

Cantata, Der Himmel lacht! die Erde jubiliert (1715)   **BWV31**

Cantata, Liebster Jesu, mein Verlangen, dialogue (1726)   **BWV32**

Cantata, Allein zu dir, Herr Jesu Christ, chorale (1724)   **BWV33**

Cantata, O ewiges Feuer, O Ursprung der Liebe (1740s)   **BWV34**

Cantata, O ewiges Feuer, O Ursprung der Liebe (1726)   **BWV34***a*

Cantata, Geist und Seele wird verwirret (1726)   **BWV35**

Cantata, Schwingt freudig euch empor (1731)   **BWV36**

Cantata, Steigt freudig in die Luft (1726)   **BWV36***a*

Cantata, Die Freude reget sich (?1735)   **BWV36***b*

BWV36c	Cantata, Schwingt freudig euch empor (1725)
BWV37	Cantata, Wer da gläubet und getauft wird (1724)
BWV38	Cantata, Aus tiefer Not schrei ich zu dir, chorale (1724)
BWV39	Cantata, Brich dem Hungrigen dein Brot (1726)
BWV40	Cantata, Dazu ist erschienen der Sohn Gottes (1723)
BWV41	Cantata, Jesu, nun sei gepreiset, chorale (1725)
BWV42	Cantata, Am Abend aber desselbigen Sabbats (1725)
BWV43	Cantata, Gott fähret auf mit Jauchzen (1726)
BWV44	Cantata, Sie werden euch in die Bann tun (1724)
BWV45	Cantata, Es ist dir gesagt, Mensch, was gut ist (1726)
BWV46	Cantata, Schauet doch und sehet (1723)
BWV47	Cantata, Wer sich selbst erhöhet (1726)
BWV48	Cantata, Ich elender Mensch, wer wird mich erlösen (1723)
BWV49	Cantata, Ich geh und suche mit Verlangen, dialogue (1726)
BWV50	Cantata, Nun ist das Heil und die Kraft
BWV51	Cantata, Jauchzet Gott in allen Landen! (?1730)
BWV52	Cantata, Falsche Welt, dir trau ich nicht (1726)
BWV54	Cantata, Widerstehe doch der Sünde (?1714)
BWV55	Cantata, Ich armer Mensch, ich Sündenknecht (1726)
BWV56	Cantata, Ich will den Kreuzstab gerne tragen (1726)
BWV57	Cantata, Selig ist der Mann, dialogue (1725)
BWV58	Cantata, Ach Gott, wie manches Herzeleid, dialogue (1727)

Cantata, Wer mich liebet, der wird mein Wort halten (1723–4)	BWV59
Cantata, O Ewigkeit, du Donnerwort, dialogue (1723)	BWV60
Cantata, Nun komm, der Heiden Heiland (1714)	BWV61
Cantata, Nun komm, der Heiden Heiland, chorale (1724)	BWV62
Cantata, Christen ätzet diesen Tag (before 1716)	BWV63
Cantata, Sehet welch eine Liebe (1723)	BWV64
Cantata, Sie werden aus Saba alle kommen (1724)	BWV65
Cantata, Erfreut euch, ihr Herzen, dialogue (?1724)	BWV66
Cantata, Der Himmel dacht auf Anhalts Ruhm und Glück(1718)	BWV66*a*
Cantata, Halt im Gedächtnis Jesum Christ (1724)	BWV67
Cantata, Also hat Gott die Welt geliebt (1725)	BWV68
Cantata, Lobe den Herrn, meine Seele (1740s)	BWV69
Cantata, Lobe den Herrn, meine Seele (1723)	BWV69*a*
Cantata, Wachet! betet! betet! wachet! (1723)	BWV70
Cantata, Wachet! betet! betet! wachet! (1716)	BWV70*a*
Cantata, Gott ist mein König (1708)	BWV71
Cantata, Alles nur nach Gottes Willen (1726)	BWV72
Cantata, Herr, wie du willt, so schicks mit mir (1724)	BWV73
Cantata, Wer mich liebet, der wird mein Wort halten (1725)	BWV74
Cantata, Die Elenden sollen essen (1723)	BWV75
Cantata, Die Himmel erzählen die Ehre Gottes (1723)	BWV76

BWV77	Cantata, Du sollt Gott, deinen Herren, lieben (1723)
BWV78	Cantata, Jesu, der du meine Seele, chorale (1724)
BWV79	Cantata, Gott der Herr ist Sonn und Schild (1725)
BWV80	Cantata, Ein feste Burg ist unser Gott (?1724)
BWV80*a*	Cantata, Alles, was von Gott geboren (1715)
BWV80*b*	Cantata, Ein feste Burg ist unser Gott (1723)
BWV81	Cantata, Jesus schläft, was soll ich hoffen? (1724)
BWV82	Cantata, Ich habe genug (1727)
BWV83	Cantata, Erfreute Zeit im neuen Bunde (1724)
BWV84	Cantata, Ich bin vergnügt mit meinem Glücke (1727)
BWV85	Cantata, Ich bin ein guter Hirt (1725)
BWV86	Cantata, Wahrlich, wahrlich, ich sage euch (1724)
BWV87	Cantata, Bisher habt ihr nichts gebeten (1725)
BWV88	Cantata, Siehe, ich will viel Fischer aussenden (1726)
BWV89	Cantata, Was soll ich aus dir machen, Ephraim? (1723)
BWV90	Cantata, Es reisset euch ein schrecklich Ende (1723)
BWV91	Cantata, Gelobet seist du, Jesu Christ, chorale (1724)
BWV92	Cantata, Ich hab in Gottes Herz und Sinn, chorale (1725)
BWV93	Cantata, Wer nur den lieben Gott lässt walten, chorale (1724)
BWV94	Cantata, Was frag ich nach der Welt, chorale (1724)
BWV95	Cantata, Christus, der ist mein Leben, chorale (1723)
BWV96	Cantata, Herr Christ, der einge Gottessohn, chorale (1724)
BWV97	Cantata, In allen meinen Taten, chorale (1734)
BWV98	Cantata, Was Gott tut, das ist wohlgetan (1726)

Cantata, Was Gott tut, das ist wohlgetan, chorale (1724)	BWV99
Cantata, Was Gott tut, das ist wohlgetan, chorale (1732–5)	BWV100
Cantata, Nimm von uns, Herr, du treuer Gott, chorale (1724)	BWV101
Cantata, Herr, deine Augen sehen nach dem Glauben (1726)	BWV102
Cantata, Ihr werdet weinen und heulen (1725)	BWV103
Cantata, Du Hirte Israel, höre (1724)	BWV104
Cantata, Herr, gehe nicht ins Gericht (1723)	BWV105
Cantata, Gottes Zeit ist die allerbeste Zeit, Actus tragicus (?1707)	BWV106
Cantata, Was willst du dich betrüben, chorale (1724)	BWV107
Cantata, Es ist euch gut, dass ich hingehe (1725)	BWV108
Cantata, Ich glaube, lieber Herr, hilf meinem Ünglauben! (1723)	BWV109
Cantata, Unser Mund sei voll Lachens (1725)	BWV110
Cantata, Was mein Gott will, das g'scheh allzeit, chorale (1725)	BWV111
Cantata, Der Herr ist mein getreuer Hirt, chorale (1731)	BWV112
Cantata, Herr Jesu Christ, du höchstes Gut, chorale (1724)	BWV113
Cantata, Ach, lieben Christen, seid getrost, chorale (1724)	BWV114
Cantata, Mache dich, mein Geist, bereit, chorale (1724)	BWV115
Cantata, Du Friedefürst, Herr Jesu Christ, chorale (1724)	BWV116
Cantata, Sei Lob und Ehr dem höchsten Gut, chorale (c.1728–31)	BWV117
Motet, O Jesu Christ, mein Lebens Licht, chorale (1736–7)	BWV118
Cantata, Preise, Jerusalem, den Herrn (1723)	BWV119

BWV120	Cantata, Gott, man lobet dich in der Stille (1728–9)
BWV120*a*	Cantata, Herr Gott, Beherrscher aller Dinge (?1729)
BWV120*b*	Cantata, Gott, man lobet dich in der Stille (1730)
BWV121	Cantata, Christum wir sollen loben schon, chorale (1724)
BWV122	Cantata, Das neugeborne Kindelein, chorale (1724)
BWV123	Cantata, Liebster Immanuel, Herzog der Frommen, chorale (1725)
BWV124	Cantata, Meinen Jesum lass ich nicht, chorale (1725)
BWV125	Cantata, Mit Fried und Freud ich fahr dahin, chorale (1725)
BWV126	Cantata, Erhalt uns, Herr, bei deinem Wort, chorale (1725)
BWV127	Cantata, Herr Jesu Christ, wahr' Mesnch und Gott, chorale (1725)
BWV128	Cantata, Auf Christi Himmelfahrt allein (1725)
BWV129	Cantata, Gelobet sei der Herr, mein Gott, chorale (1726–7)
BWV130	Cantata, Herr Gott, dich loben alle wir, chorale (1724)
BWV131	Cantata, Aus der Tiefen rufe ich, Herr, zu dir (1707)
BWV132	Cantata, Bereitet die Wege, bereitet die Bahn! (1715)
BWV133	Cantata, Ich freue mich in dir, chorale (1724)
BWV134	Cantata, Ein Herz, das seinen Jesum lebend (1724)
BWV134*a*	Cantata, Die Zeit, die Tag und Jahre macht (1719)
BWV135	Cantata, Ach Herr, mich armen Sünder, chorale (1724)
BWV136	Cantata, Erforsche mich, Gott, und erfahre mein Herz (1723)
BWV137	Cantata, Lobe den Herren, den mächtigen König der Ehren, chorale (1725)

Cantata, Warum betrübst du dich, mein Herz?, BWV138
chorale (1723)

Cantata, Wohl dem, der sich auf seinen Gott, BWV139
chorale (1724)

Cantata, Wachet auf, ruft uns die Stimme, BWV140
chorale (1731)

Cantata, Nimm, was dein ist, und gehe hin (1724) BWV144

Cantata, Ich lebe, mein Herze, zu deinem, BWV145
Ergötzen (?1729)

Cantata, Wir müssen durch viel Trübsal (c.1726–8) BWV146

Cantata, Herz und Mund und Tat und Leben (1723) BWV147

Cantata, Herz und Mund und Tat und Leben (1716) BWV147*a*

Cantata, Bringet dem Herrn Ehre seines Namens (?1723) BWV148

Cantata, Man singet mit Freuden vom Sieg (1728–9) BWV149

Cantata, Nach dir, Herr, verlanget mich (c.1708–9) BWV150

Cantata, Süsser Trost, mein Jesus kömmt (1725) BWV151

Cantata, Tritt auf die Glaubensbahn (1714) BWV152

Cantata, Schau, lieber Gott, wie meine Feind (1724) BWV153

Cantata, Mein liebster Jesus ist verloren (1724) BWV154

Cantata, Mein Gott, wie lang, ach lange (1716) BWV155

Cantata, Ich steh mit einem Fuss im Grabe (?1729) BWV156

Cantata, Ich lasse dich nicht, BWV157
du segnest mich denn (1727)

Cantata, Der Friede sei mit dir BWV158

BWV159	Cantata, Sehet, wir gehn hinauf gen Jerusalem (?1729)
BWV161	Cantata, Komm, du süsse Todesstunde (1715)
BWV162	Cantata, Ach! ich sehe, jetzt, da ich zur Hochzeit gehe (1715)
BWV163	Cantata, Nur jedem das Seine (1715)
BWV164	Cantata, Ihr, die ihr eich von Christo nennet (1725)
BWV165	Cantata, O heilges Geist- und Wasserbad (1715)
BWV166	Cantata, Wo gehest du hin? (1724)
BWV167	Cantata, Ihr Menschen, rühmet Gottes Liebe (1723)
BWV168	Cantata, Tue Rechnung! Donnerwort (1725)
BWV169	Cantata, Gott soll allein mein Herze haben (1726)
BWV170	Cantata, Vergnügte Ruh', eliebte Seelenlust (1726)
BWV171	Cantata, Gott, wie dein Name, so ist auch dein Ruhm (?1729)
BWV172	Cantata, Erschallet, ihr Lieder (1714)
BWV173	Cantata, Erhöhtes Fliesch und Blut (?1724)
BWV173a	Cantata, Durchlauchtster Leopold, serenata (?c.1722)
BWV174	Cantata, Ich liebe den Höchsten von ganzem Gemüte (1729)
BWV175	Cantata, Er rufet seinen Schafen mit Namen (1725)
BWV176	Cantata, Es ist ein trotzig, und verzagt Ding (1725)
BWV177	Cantata, Ich ruf zu dir, Herr Jesu Christ, chorale (1732)
BWV178	Cantata, Wo Gott der Herr nicht bei uns hält, chorale (1724)
BWV179	Cantata, Siehe zu, dass deine Gottesfurcht (1723)
BWV180	Cantata, Schmücke dich, o liebe Seele, chorale (1724)
BWV181	Cantata, Leichtgesinnte Flattergeister (1724)

Cantata, Himmelskönig, sei willkommen (1714)	BWV182
Cantata, Sie werden euch in den Bann tun (1725)	BWV183
Cantata, Erwünschtes Freudenlicht (1724)	BWV184
Cantata (?1722–3)	BWV184*a*
Cantata, Barmherziges Herze der ewigen Liebe (1715)	BWV185
Cantata, Ärgre dich, o Seele, nicht (1723)	BWV186
Cantata, Ärgre dich, o Seele, nicht (1716)	BWV186*a*
Cantata, Es wartet alles auf dich (1726)	BWV187
Cantata, Ich habe meine Zuversicht (c.1728)	BWV188
Cantata, Singet dem Herrn ein neues Lied! (1724)	BWV190
Cantata, Singet dem Herrn ein neues Lied! (1730)	BWV190*a*
Cantata, Gloria in exclesis Deo (1740s)	BWV191
Cantata, Nun danket alle Gott, chorale (1730)	BWV192
Cantata, Ihr Tore zu Zion (c.1727)	BWV193
Cantata, Ihr Häuser des Himmels, ihr scheinenden Lichter (1727)	BWV193*a*
Cantata, Höchsterwünschtes Freudenfest (1723)	BWV194
Cantata, (before 1723)	BWV194*a*
Cantata, Dem Gerechten muss das Licht (c. 1737)	BWV195
Cantata, Der Herr denket an uns (?1708)	BWV196
Cantata, Gott ist unsre Zuversicht (c.1742)	BWV197
Cantata, Ehre sei Gott in der Höhe (c.1728)	BWV197*a*
Cantata, Trauer Ode: Lass, Fürstin, lass noch einen Strahl (1727)	BWV198

BWV199	Cantata, Mein Herze schwimmt im Blut (1714)
BWV200	Cantata, Bekennen will ich seinen Namen (?c.1742)
BWV201	Cantata, Der Streit zwischen Phoebus und Pan (?1729)
BWV202	Cantata, Weichet nur, betrübte Schatten (?1718–23)
BWV204	Cantata, Ich bin in mir vergnügt (1726–7)
BWV205	Cantata, Der zufriedengestellte Äolus, dramma per musica (1725)
BWV205*a*	Cantata, Blast Lärmen, ihr Feinde! (1734)
BWV206	Cantata, Schleicht, spielende Wellen, dramma per musica (1736)
BWV207	Cantata, Vereinigte Zwietracht der wechselnden Saiten, dramma per musica (1726)
BWV207*a*	Cantata, Auf, schmetternde Töne, dramma per musica (?1735)
BWV208	Cantata, Was mir behagt, ist nur die muntre Jagd! (?1713)
BWV208*a*	Cantata, Was mir behagt, ist nur die muntre Jagd! (1740–2)
BWV209	Cantata, Non sa che sia dolore (?1734)
BWV210	Cantata, O holder Tag, erwünschte Zeit (c. 1740)
BWV210*a*	Cantata, O angenehme Melodei! (?1738–40)
BWV211	'Coffee' Cantata, Schweigt stille, plaudert nicht (c.1734–5)
BWV212	'Peasant' Cantata, Mer hahn en neue Oberkeet (1742)
BWV213	Cantata, Hercules auf dem Scheidewege, dramma per musica (1733)
BWV214	Cantata, Tönet, ihr Pauken! Erschallet, Trompeten!, dramma per musica (1733)

Cantata, Preise dein Glücke, gesegnetes Sachsen, dramma per musica (1734)	BWV215
Cantata, Vergnügte Pleissenstadt (1728)	BWV216
Cantata, Erwählte Pleissenstadt (c. 1728)	BWV216*a*
Cantata, Meine Seele soll Gott loben	BWV223
Motet, Singet dem Herrn ein neues Lied (?1727)	BWV225
Motet, Der Geist hilft unser Schwachheit auf (1729)	BWV226
Motet, Jesu, meine Freude (?1723)	BWV227
Motet, Fürchte dich nicht (?1726)	BWV228
Motet, Komm, Jesu, komm! (1730)	BWV229
Motet, Lobet den Herrn alle Heiden	BWV230
Mass, B minor (c.1747–9)	BWV232
Missa breve, F major (1730s)	BWV233
Kyrie, F major (1730s)	BWV233*a*
Missa breve, A major (1730s)	BWV234
Missa breve, G minor (1730s)	BWV235
Missa breve, G major (1730s)	BWV236
Sanctus, C major (1723)	BWV237
Sanctus, D major (?1723)	BWV238
Sanctus, D minor (c. 1735–46)	BWV239
Sanctus, G major (c. 1735–46)	BWV240
Sanctus, D major	BWV241
Christe eleison	BWV242
Magnificat, D major (c. 1728–31)	BWV243

BWV243a	Magnificat, E♭ major (1723)
BWV244	St. Matthew Passion (c. 1727–9)
BWV244a	Cantata, Klagt, Kinder, klagt es aller Welt (1729)
BWV245	St. John Passion (1724)
BWV247	St. Mark Passion (1731)
BWV248	Christmas Oratorio (1734–5)
BWV249	Easter Oratorio (1725)
BWV249a	Cantata, Entfliehet, verschwindet, entweichet, ihr Sorgen (1725)
BWV249b	Cantata, Die Feier des Genius, dramma per music (1726)
BWV250	Wedding chorale, Was Gott tut das ist wohlgetan
BWV251	Wedding chorale, Sei Lob und Ehr' dem höchsten Gut
BWV252	Wedding chorale, Nun danket alle Gott
BWV253	Chorale, Ach bleibe bei uns, Herr Jesu Christ
BWV254	Chorale, Ach Gott, erhör' mein Seufzen
BWV255	Chorale, Ach Gott und Herr
BWV256	Chorale, Ach lieben Christen, seid getrost
BWV257	Chorale, Wär' Gott nicht mit uns diese Zeit
BWV258	Chorale, Wo Gott der Herr nicht bei uns hält
BWV259	Chorale, Ach, was soll ich Sünder machen
BWV260	Chorale, Allein Gott in der Höh' sei Ehr'
BWV261	Chorale, Allein zu dir, Herr Jesu Christ
BWV262	Chorale, Alle Menschen müssen sterben
BWV263	Chorale, Alles ist an Gottes Segen

BWV288	Chorale, Das alte Jahr vergangen ist
BWV289	Chorale, Das alte Jahr vergangen ist
BWV290	Chorale, Das walt' Gott Vater und Gott Sohn
BWV291	Chorale, Das walt' mein Gott, Vater, Sohn und heiliger Geist
BWV292	Chorale, Den Vater dort oben
BWV293	Chorale, Der du bist drei in Einigkeit
BWV294	Chorale, Der Tag, der ist so freudenreich
BWV295	Chorale, Des heil'gen Geistes reiche Gnad'
BWV296	Chorale, Die Nacht ist kommen
BWV297	Chorale, Die Sonn' hat sich mit ihrem Glanz
BWV298	Chorale, Dies sind die heil'gen zehn Gebot'
BWV299	Chorale, Dir, dir, Jehova, will ich singen
BWV300	Chorale, Du grosser Schmerzensmann
BWV301	Chorale, Du, o shönes Welgebäude
BWV302	Chorale, Ein' feste Burg ist unser Gott
BWV303	Chorale, Ein' feste Burg ist unser Gott
BWV304	Chorale, Eins ist Not! ach Herr, dies Eine
BWV305	Chorale, Erbarm' dich mein, o Herre Gott
BWV306	Chorale, Erstanden ist der heil'ge Christ
BWV307	Chorale, Es ist gewisslich an der Zeit
BWV308	Chorale, Es spricht der Unweisen Mund wohl
BWV309	Chorale, Es stehn vor Gottes Throne
BWV310	Chorale, Es wird schier der letzte Tag herkommen

BWV336	Chorale, Herr Jesu Christ, wahr'r Mensch und Gott
BWV337	Chorale, Herr, nun lass in Frieden
BWV338	Chorale, Herr, straf mich nicht in deinem Zorn
BWV339	Chorale, Herr, wie du willst, so schick's mit mir
BWV340	Chorale, Herzlich lieb hab ich dich, o Herr
BWV341	Chorale, Heut' ist, o Mensch, ein grosser Trauertag
BWV342	Chorale, Heut' triumphieret Gottes Sohn
BWV343	Chorale, Hilf, Gott, dass mir's gelinge
BWV344	Chorale, Hilf, Herr Jesu, lass gelingen
BWV345	Chorale, Ich bin ja, Herr, in deiner Macht
BWV346	Chorale, Ich dank' dir, Gott, für all' Wohltat
BWV347	Chorale, Ich dank' dir, lieber Herre
BWV348	Chorale, Ich dank' dir, lieber Herre
BWV349	Chorale, Ich dank' dir schon durch deinen Sohn
BWV350	Chorale, Ich danke dir, o Gott, in einem Throne
BWV351	Chorale, Ich hab' mein' Sach' Gott heimgestellt
BWV352	Chorale, Jesu, der du meine Seele
BWV353	Chorale, Jesu, der du meine Seele
BWV354	Chorale, Jesu, der du meine Seele
BWV355	Chorale, Jesu, der du selbsten wohl
BWV356	Chorale, Jesu, du mein liebstes Leben
BWV357	Chorale, Jesu, Jesu, du bist mein
BWV358	Chorale, Jesu, meine Freude
BWV359	Chorale, Jesu meiner Seelen Wonne

BWV384	Chorale, Nicht so traurig, nicht so sehr
BWV385	Chorale, Nun bitten wir den heiligen Geist
BWV386	Chorale, Nun danket alle Gott
BWV387	Chorale, Nun freut euch, Gottes Kinder all'
BWV388	Chorale, Nun freut euch, lieben Christen, g'mein
BWV389	Chorale, Nun lob', mein' Seel', den Herren
BWV390	Chorale, Nun lob', mein' Seel', den Herren
BWV391	Chorale, Nun preiset alle Gottes Barmherzigkeit
BWV392	Chorale, Nun ruhen alle Wälder
BWV393	Chorale, O Welt, sieh hier dein Leben
BWV394	Chorale, O Welt, sieh hier dein Leben
BWV395	Chorale, O Welt, sieh hier dein Leben
BWV396	Chorale, Nun sich der Tag geendet hat
BWV397	Chorale, O Ewigkeit, du Donnerwort
BWV398	Chorale, O Gott du frommer Gott
BWV399	Chorale, O Gott du frommer Gott
BWV400	Chorale, O Herzensangst, o Bangigkeit
BWV401	Chorale, O Lamm Gottes, unschuldig
BWV402	Chorale, O Mensch, bewein' dein' Sünde gross
BWV403	Chorale, O Mensch, schau Jesum Christum an
BWV404	Chorale, O Traurigkeit, o Herzeleid
BWV405	Chorale, O wie selig seid ihr doch, ihr Frommen
BWV406	Chorale, O wie selig seid ihr doch, ihr Frommen
BWV407	Chorale, Ô wir armen Sünder

BWV432	Chorale, Wenn wir in höchsten Nöten sein
BWV433	Chorale, Wer Gott vertraut, hat wohl gebaut
BWV434	Chorale, Wer nur den lieben Gott lässt walten
BWV435	Chorale, Wie bist du, Seele, in mir so gar betrübt
BWV436	Chorale, Wie schön leuchtet der Morgenstern
BWV437	Chorale, Wir glauben all' an einen Gott
BWV438	Chorale, Wo Gott zum Haus nicht gibt sein' Gunst
BWV439	Chorale, Ach, dass nicht die letzte Stunde
BWV440	Chorale, Auf, auf! die rechte Zeit ist hier
BWV441	Chorale, Auf, auf! mein Herz, mit Freuden
BWV442	Chorale, Beglückteter Stand getreuer Seelen
BWV443	Chorale, Beschränkt, ihr Weisen dieser Welt
BWV444	Chorale, Brich entzwei, mein armes Herze
BWV445	Chorale, Brunnquell aller Güter
BWV446	Chorale, Der lieben Sonnen Licht und Pracht
BWV447	Chorale, Der Tag ist hin, die Sonne gehet nieder
BWV448	Chorale, Der Tag mit seinem Lichte
BWV449	Chorale, Dich bet'ich an, mein höchster Gott
BWV450	Chorale, Die bittre Leidenszeit beginnet abermal
BWV451	Chorale, Die goldne Sonne, voll Freud' und Wonne
BWV452	Chorale, Dir, dir Jehovan, will ich singen
BWV453	Chorale, Eins ist Not! ach Herr, dies Eine
BWV454	Chorale, Ermuntre dich, mein schwacher Geist
BWV455	Chorale, Erwürgtes Lamm, das die verwahrten Siegel

BWV480	Chorale, Kommt wieder aus der finstern Gruft
BWV481	Chorale, Lasset uns mit Jesu ziehen
BWV482	Chorale, Liebes Herz, bedenke doch
BWV483	Chorale, Liebster Gott, wann werd' ich sterben?
BWV484	Chorale, Liebster Herr Jesu! wo bleibest du so lange?
BWV485	Chorale, Liebster Immanuel, Merzog der Frommen
BWV486	Chorale, Mein Jesu, dem die Seraphinen
BWV487	Chorale, Mein Jesu? was für Seelenweh
BWV488	Chorale, Meines Lebens letzte Zeit
BWV489	Chorale, Nicht so traurig nicht so sehr
BWV490	Chorale, Nur mein Jesus ist mein Leben
BWV491	Chorale, O du Liebe meine Liebe
BWV492	Chorale, O finstre Nacht
BWV493	Chorale, O Jesulein süss, o Jesulein mild
BWV494	Chorale, O liebe Seele, zieh' die Sinnen
BWV495	Chorale, O wie selig seid ihr doch, ihr Frommen
BWV496	Chorale, Seelen-Bräutigam, Jesu, Gottes Lamm!
BWV497	Chorale, Seelenweide, meine Freude
BWV498	Chorale, Selig, wer an Jesum denkt
BWV499	Chorale, Sei gegrüsset, Jesu gütig
BWV500	Chorale, So gehst du nun, mein Jesu, hin
BWV501	Chorale, So giebst du nun, mein Jesu, gute Nacht
BWV502	Chorale, So wünsch' ich mir zu guter Letz
BWV503	Chorale, Steh' ich bei meinem Gott

BWV534	Prelude and fugue, organ, F minor (1708–17)
BWV535	Prelude and fugue, organ, G minor (1708–17)
BWV536	Prelude and fugue, organ, A major (1708–17)
BWV537	Fantasia and fugue, organ, C minor (1708–17)
BWV538	Toccata and fugue, organ, 'Dorian', D minor (1708–17)
BWV539	Prelude and fugue, organ, D minor (1720s)
BWV540	Toccata and fugue, organ, F major (1708–17)
BWV541	Prelude and fugue, organ, G major (1708–17)
BWV542	Fantasia and fugue, organ, G minor (1708–23)
BWV543	Prelude and fugue, organ, A minor (1708–17)
BWV544	Prelude and fugue, organ, B minor (1727–31)
BWV545	Prelude and fugue, organ, C major (1708–17)
BWV546	Prelude and fugue, organ, C minor (1708–17)
BWV547	Prelude and fugue, organ, C major (after 1723)
BWV548	Prelude and fugue, organ, E minor (1727–31)
BWV549	Prelude and fugue, organ, C minor (1708–17)
BWV550	Prelude and fugue, organ, G major (before 1708)
BWV551	Prelude and fugue, organ, A minor (before 1708)
BWV552	Prelude and fugue, organ, 'St. Anne', E♭ major, Clavier-Übung, iii (1739)
BWV562	Fantasia and fugue, organ, C minor (1708–17; c.1745)
BWV563	Fantasia, organ, B minor (before 1707)
BWV564	Toccata, adagio and fugue, organ, C major (1708–17)
BWV565	Toccata and fugue, organ, D minor (before 1708)

Prelude and fugue, organ, E major (before 1708)	**BWV566**
Prelude, organ, G major (before 1708)	**BWV568**
Prelude, organ, A minor (before 1708)	**BWV569**
Fantasia, organ, C major (before 1707)	**BWV570**
Fantasia, organ, G major (before 1708)	**BWV572**
Fantasia, organ, C major, Clavierbüchlein, i, for Anna Magdalena Bach (c. 1722)	**BWV573**
Fugue on theme by Legrenzi, C minor	**BWV574**
Fugue, organ, C minor (?1708–17)	**BWV575**
Fugue, organ, G minor (?1707)	**BWV578**
Fugue on theme by Corelli, B minor	**BWV579**
Passacaglia, organ, C minor	**BWV582**
Trio, organ, D minor	**BWV583**
Trio, organ, G major	**BWV586**
Aria, organ, F major	**BWV587**
Canzona, organ, D minor (c. 1715)	**BWV588**
Pastorale, organ, F major (c. 1710)	**BWV590**
Organ concerto, G major (1708–17)	**BWV592**
Organ concerto, A minor (1708–17)	**BWV593**
Organ concerto, C major (1708–17)	**BWV594**
Organ concerto, C major (1708–17)	**BWV595**
Organ concerto, D minor (1708–17)	**BWV596**
Organ concerto, E♭ major (1708–17)	**BWV597**
Pedal-Exercitium for organ	**BWV598**

BWV599	Nun komm' der Heiden Heiland,
	Das Orgel-Büchlein (c. 1713–17)
BWV600	Gott, durch deine Güte,
	Das Orgel-Büchlein (c. 1713–17)
BWV601	Herr Christ, der ein'ge Gottes-Sohn,
	Das Orgel-Büchlein (c. 1713-17)
BWV602	Lob sei dem allmächtigen Gott,
	Das Orgel-Büchlein (c.1713–17)
BWV603	Puer natus in Bethlehem,
	Das Orgel-Büchlein (c. 1713–17)
BWV604	Gelobet seist du, Jesu Christ,
	Das Orgel-Büchlein (c.1713–17)
BWV605	Der Tag, der ist so freudenreich,
	Das Orgel-Büchlein (c.1713–17)
BWV606	Vom Himmel hoch da komm' ich her,
	Das Orgel-Büchlein (c.1713–17)
BWV607	Vom Himmel kam der Engel Schar,
	Das Orgel-Büchlein (c.1713–17)
BWV608	In dulci jubilo, Das Orgel-Büchlein (c.1713–17)
BWV609	Lobt Gott, ihr Christen, allzugleich,
	Das Orgel-Büchlein (c.1713–17)
BWV610	Jesu, meine Freude, Das Orgel-Büchlein (c.1713–17)
BWV611	Christum wir sollen loben schon,
	Das Orgel-Büchlein (c.1713–17)

Wir Christenleut', Das Orgel-Büchlein (c.1713–17) BWV612

Helft mir Gottes Güte preisen, BWV613
Das Orgel-Büchlein (c.1713–17)

Das alte Jahr vergangen ist, BWV614
Das Orgel-Büchlein (1740s)

In dir ist Freude, Das Orgel-Büchlein (c. 1713–17) BWV615

Mit Fried' und Freud' ich fahr dahin, BWV616
Das Orgel-Büchlein (c. 1713–17)

Herr Gott, nun schleuss den Himmel auf, BWV617
Das Orgel-Büchlein (c.1713–17)

O Lamm Gottes unschuldig, BWV618
Das Orgel-Büchlein (c. 1713–17)

Christe, du Lamm Gottes, BWV619
Das Orgel-Büchlein (c. 1713–17)

Christus, der uns selig macht, BWV620
Das Orgel-Büchlein (c.1713–17)

Da Jesus an dem Kreuze stund', BWV621
Das Orgel-Büchlein (c.1713–17)

O Mensch, bewein' dein' Sünde gross, BWV622
Das Orgel-Büchlein (c. 1713–17)

Wir danken dir, Herr Jesu Christ, BWV623
Das Orgel-Büchlein (c.1713–17)

Elf Gott, dass mir's gelinge, BWV624
Das Orgel-Büchlein (c. 1713–17)

BWV625	Christ lag in Todesbanden, Das Orgel-Büchlein (c. 1713–17)
BWV626	Jesus Christus, unser Heiland, Das Orgel-Büchlein (c.1713–17)
BWV627	Christ ist erstanden, Das Orgel-Büchlein (c. 1713–17)
BWV628	Erstanden ist der heil'ge Christ, Das Orgel-Büchlein (c.1713–17)
BWV629	Erschienen ist der herrliche Tag, Das Orgel-Büchlein (c.1713–17)
BWV630	Heut' triumphieret Gottes Sohn, Das Orgel-Büchlein (c.1713–17)
BWV631	Komm, Gott Schöpfer, heiliger Geist, Das Orgel-Büchlein (c. 1713–17)
BWV632	Herr Jesu Christ, dich zu uns wend', Das Orgel-Büchlein (c. 1713–17)
BWV633	Liebster Jesu, wir sind hier, Das Orgel-Büchlein (c. 1713–17)
BWV635	Dies sind die heil'gen zehn Gebot', Das Orgel-Büchlein (c.1713–17)
BWV636	Vater unser im Himmelreich, Das Orgel-Büchlein (c. 1713–17)
BWV637	Drch Adam's Fall ist ganz verderbt, Das Orgel-Büchlein (c.1713–17)
BWV638	Es ist das Heil uns kommen her, Das Orgel-Büchlein (c.1713–17)

BWV651	Chorale, Fantasia super Komm, Heiliger Geist (1708–17)
BWV652	Chorale, Komm, Heiliger Geist (1708–17)
BWV653	Chorale, An Wasserflüssen Babylon (1708–17)
BWV654	Chorale, Schmücke, dich, o liebe Seele (1708–17)
BWV655	Chorale, Trio super Herr Jesu Christ, dich zu uns wend (1708–17)
BWV656	Chorale, O Lamm Gottes unschuldig (1708–17)
BWV657	Chorale, Nun danket alle Gott (1708–17)
BWV658	Chorale, Von Gott will ich nicht lassen (1708–17)
BWV659	Chorale, Nun komm, der Heiden Heiland (1708–17)
BWV660	Chorale, Trio super Nun komm, der Heiden Heiland (1708–17)
BWV661	Chorale, Nun komm, der Heiden Heiland (1708–17)
BWV662	Chorale, Allein Gott in der Höh sei Ehr (1708–17)
BWV663	Chorale, Allein Gott in der Höh sei Ehr (1708–17)
BWV664	Chorale, Trio super Allein Gott in der Höh sei Ehr (1708–17)
BWV665	Chorale, Jesus Christus, unser Heiland (1708–17)
BWV666	Chorale, Jesus Christus, unser Heiland (1708-17)
BWV667	Chorale, Komm, Gott, Schöpfer, Heiliger Geist (1708-17)
BWV668	Chorale, Wenn wir in hoechsten Noeten sein (c. 1744–7)
BWV669	Kyrie, Gott Vater in Ewigkeit, Chorale prelude in Clavier- Übung, iii (1739)
BWV670	Christe, aller Welt Trost, Chorale prelude in Clavier-Übung, iii (1739)
BWV671	Kyrie, Gott heiliger Geist, Chorale prelude in Clavier-Übung, iii (1739)

Kyrie, Gott Vater in Ewigkeit, Chorale prelude in Clavier-Übung, iii (1739)	BWV672
Christe, aller Welt Trost, Chorale prelude in Clavier-Übung, iii (1739)	BWV673
Kyrie, Gott heiliger Geist, Chorale prelude in Clavier-Übung, iii (1739)	BWV674
Allein Gott in der Höh sei Ehr, Chorale prelude in Clavier-Übung, iii (1739)	BWV675
Allein Gott in der Höh sei Ehr, Chorale prelude in Clavier-Übung, iii (1739)	BWV676
Fughetta super Allein Gott in der Höh sei Ehr, Chorale prelude in Clavier-Übung, iii (1739)	BWV677
Dies sind die heilgen zehen Gebot, Chorale prelude in Clavier-Übung, iii (1739)	BWV678
Fughetta super Dies sind die heiligen zeben Gebot, Chorale prelude in Clavier-Übung, iii (1739)	BWV679
Wir gläuben all an einen Gott, Chorale prelude in Clavier-Übung, iii (1739)	BWV680
Fughetta super Wir gläuben all an einen Gott, Chorale prelude in Clavier-Übung, iii (1739)	BWV681
Vater unser im Himmelreich, Chorale prelude in Clavier-Übung, iii (1739)	BWV682
Vater unser im Himmelreich, Chorale prelude in Clavier-Übung, iii (1739)	BWV683

BWV684	Christ, unser Herr, zum Jordan kam, Chorale prelude in Clavier-Übung, iii (1739)
BWV685	Christ, unser Herr, zum Jordan kam, Chorale prelude in Clavier-Übung, iii (1739)
BWV686	Aus tiefer Not schrei ich zu dir, Chorale prelude in Clavier-Übung, iii (1739)
BWV687	Aus tiefer Not schrei ich zu dir, Chorale prelude in Clavier-Übung, iii (1739)
BWV688	Jesus Christus, unser Heiland, der von uns den Zorn Gottes wandt, Chorale prelude in Clavier-Übung, iii (1739)
BWV689	Fuga super Jesus Christus unser Heiland, Chorale prelude in Clavier-Übung, iii (1739)
BWV690	Wer nur den lieben Gott lässt walten (1708–17)
BWV691	Wer nur den lieben Gott lässt walten, Clavier-Büchlien for W. F. Bach (1720–)
BWV694	Wo soll ich fliehen hin (before 1708)
BWV695	Fantasia super Christ lag in Todes Banden (?1708–17)
BWV696	Christum wir sollen loben schon (?1708–17)
BWV697	Gelobet seist du, Jesu Christ (?1708–17)
BWV698	Herr Christ, der einig Gottes Sohn (?1708–17)
BWV699	Nun komm, der Heiden Heiland (?1708–17)
BWV700	Vom Himmel hoch, da komm ich her (?1708)
BWV701	Vom Himmel hoch, da komm ich her (?1708–17)
BWV703	Gottes Sohn ist kommen (?1708–17)

Lob sei dem allmächtigen Gott (?1708–17)	**BWV704**
Liebster Jesu, wir sind hier (1708–17)	**BWV706**
Herr Jesu Christ, dich zu uns wend (?1708–17)	**BWV709**
Wir Christenleut habn jetzund Freud (?1708–17)	**BWV710**
Allein Gott in der Höh sei Ehr (?1708–17)	**BWV711**
In dich hab ich gehoffet, Herr (?1708–17)	**BWV712**
Fantasia super Jesu, meine Freud (?1708–17)	**BWV713**
Ach Gott und Herr (?1708–17)	**BWV714**
Allein Gott in der Höh sei Ehr (1703–8 or 1708–17)	**BWV715**
Allein Gott in der Höh sei Ehr (1708–17)	**BWV717**
Christ lag in Todes Banden (before 1708)	**BWV718**
Ein feste Burg ist unser Gott (1709)	**BWV720**
Erbarm dich mein, o Herre Gott (?1708–17)	**BWV721**
Gelobet seist du, Jesu Christ (1703–8 or 1708–17)	**BWV722**
Gott, durch deine Güte (Gottes Sohn ist kommen) (before 1708)	**BWV724**
Herr Gott dich loben wir (?1708–17)	**BWV725**
Herr Jesu Christ, dich zu uns wend (1708–17)	**BWV726**
Herzlich tut mich verlangen (?1708–17)	**BWV727**
Jesus, meine Zuversicht, Clavierbüchlien, i, for Anna Magdalena Bach (c.1722)	**BWV728**
In dulci jubilo (?1708–17)	**BWV729**
Liebster Jesu, wir sind hier (?1708–17)	**BWV730**
Liebster Jesu, wir sind hier (?1708–17)	**BWV731**
Lobt Gott, ihr Christen, allzugleich (1703–8 or 1708–17)	**BWV732**

BWV733	Meine Seele erhebet den Herren
	(Fuge über das Magnificat) (1708–17)
BWV734*a*	Nun freut euch, lieben Christen gmein (?1708–17)
	O Lamm Gottes, unschuldig (1708–17)
BWV735	Fantasia super Valet will ich dir geben (1723)
BWV736	Valet will ich dir geben (1708–17)
BWV737	Vater unser im Himmelreich (?1708–17)
BWV738	Vom Himmel hoch, da komm ich her (?1708–17)
BWV739	Wie schön leucht't uns der Morgenstern (?1708–17)
BWV741	Ach Gott vom Himmel sieh darein (?1708)
BWV753	Jesu, meine Freude, Clavierbüchlien, i, for W. F. Bach (c.1723)
BWV764	Wie schön leuchtet uns der Morgenstern (?1708–17)
BWV766	Partite diverse, Christ der du bist der helle Tag (c.1700)
BWV767	Partite diverse, O Gott, du frommer Gott (c. 1700)
BWV768	Sei gegrüsset, Jesu gütig (c. 1700)
BWV769	Einige canonische Veränderungen über das Weynacht Lied,
	Vom Himmel hoch da komm ich her, organ (1748)
BWV772	Invention, C major, Clavier-Büchlein for W. F. Bach (1723)
BWV773	Invention, C minor, Clavier-Büchlein for W. F. Bach (1723)
BWV774	Invention, D major, Clavier-Büchlein for W. F. Bach (1723)
BWV775	Invention, D minor, Clavier-Büchlein for W. F. Bach (1723)
BWV776	Invention, E♭ major, Clavier-Büchlein for W. F. Bach (1723)
BWV777	Invention, E major, Clavier-Büchlein for W. F. Bach (1723)
BWV778	Invention, E minor, Clavier-Büchlein for W. F. Bach (1723)

Invention, F major, Clavier-Büchlein for W. F. Bach (1723)	**BWV779**
Invention, F minor, Clavier-Büchlein for W. F. Bach (1723)	**BWV780**
Invention, G major, Clavier-Büchlein for W. F. Bach (1723)	**BWV781**
Invention, G minor, Clavier-Büchlein for W. F. Bach (1723)	**BWV782**
Invention, A major, Clavier-Büchlein for W. F. Bach (1723)	**BWV783**
Invention, A minor, Clavier-Büchlein for W. F. Bach (1723)	**BWV784**
Invention, B♭ major, Clavier-Büchlein for W. F. Bach (1723)	**BWV785**
Invention, B minor, Clavier-Büchlein for W. F. Bach (1723)	**BWV786**
Sinfonia, C major, Clavier-Büchlein for W. F. Bach (1723)	**BWV787**
Sinfonia, C minor, Clavier-Büchlein for W. F. Bach (1723)	**BWV788**
Sinfonia, D major, Clavier-Büchlein for W. F. Bach (1723)	**BWV789**
Sinfonia, D minor, Clavier-Büchlein for W. F. Bach (1723)	**BWV790**
Sinfonia, E♭ major, Clavier-Büchlein for W. F. Bach (1723)	**BWV791**
Sinfonia, E major, Clavier-Büchlein for W. F. Bach (1723)	**BWV792**
Sinfonia, E minor, Clavier-Büchlein for W. F. Bach (1723)	**BWV793**
Sinfonia, F major, Clavier-Büchlein for W. F. Bach (1723)	**BWV794**
Sinfonia, F minor, Clavier-Büchlein for W. F. Bach (1723)	**BWV795**
Sinfonia, G major, Clavier-Büchlein for W. F. Bach (1723)	**BWV796**
Sinfonia, G minor, Clavier-Büchlein for W. F. Bach (1723)	**BWV797**
Sinfonia, A major, Clavier-Büchlein for W. F. Bach (1723)	**BWV798**
Sinfonia, A minor, Clavier-Büchlein for W. F. Bach (1723)	**BWV799**
Sinfonia, B♭ major, Clavier-Büchlein for W. F. Bach (1723)	**BWV800**
Sinfonia, B minor, Clavier-Büchlein for W. F. Bach (1723)	**BWV801**
Duetto, organ, E minor, Clavier-Übung (1729)	**BWV802**

BWV803	Duetto, organ, F major, Clavier-Übung (1729)
BWV804	Duetto, organ, G major, Clavier-Übung (1729)
BWV805	Duetto, organ, A minor, Clavier-Übung (1729)
BWV806	English Suite, A major (c. 1715)
BWV807	English Suite, A minor (c. 1715)
BWV808	English Suite, G minor (c. 1715)
BWV809	English Suite, F major (c. 1715)
BWV810	English Suite, E minor (c. 1715)
BWV811	English Suite, D minor (c. 1715)
BWV812	French Suite, D minor, Clavierbüchlein, i, for Anna Magdalena Bach (1722)
BWV813	French Suite, C minor, Clavierbüchlein, i, for Anna Magdalena Bach (1722)
BWV814	French Suite, B minor, Clavierbüchlein, i, for Anna Magdalena Bach (1722)
BWV815	French Suite, E♭ major, Clavierbüchlein, i, for Anna Magdalena Bach (1722)
BWV816	French Suite, G major, Clavierbüchlein, i, for Anna Magdalena Bach (1722)
BWV817	French Suite, E major, Clavierbüchlien, i, for Anna Magdalena Bach (1722)
BWV818	Suite, keyboard, A minor (c. 1722)
BWV819	Suite, keyboard, E♭ major (c. 1722)
BWV820	Ouverture, keyboard, F major (1708–14)

Suite, keyboard, B♭ major (1708–14)	BWV821
Suite, keyboard, G minor	BWV822
Suite, keyboard, F minor (1708–14)	BWV823
Partita, keyboard, B♭ major (1726–31)	BWV825
Partita, keyboard, C minor (1726–31)	BWV826
Partita, keyboard, A minor (1726–31)	BWV827
Partita, keyboard, D major (1726–31)	BWV828
Partita, keyboard, G major (1726–31)	BWV829
Partita, keyboard, E minor (1726–31)	BWV830
Ouvertüre [Partita] nach französischer Art, B minor, Clavier-Übung, ii (1735)	BWV831
Partie, keyboard, A major (1708–14)	BWV832
Prelude and partita, keyboard, F major (1708–14)	BWV833
Allemande, G minor, Clavier-Büchlien for W. F. Bach (1720–)	BWV836
Allemande, G minor, Clavier-Büchlien for W. F. Bach (1720–)	BWV837
Minuet, G major, Clavier-Büchlien for W. F. Bach (1720–)	BWV841
Minuet, G minor, Clavier-Büchlien for W. F. Bach (1720–)	BWV842
Minuet, G major, Clavier-Büchlien for W. F. Bach (1720–)	BWV843
Prelude and fugue, C major, Das wohltemperirte Clavier, i (1722)	BWV846
Prelude and fugue, C minor, Das wohltemperirte Clavier, i (1722)	BWV847
Prelude and fugue, C♯ major, Das wohltemperirte Clavier, i (1722)	BWV848

BWV849	Prelude and fugue, C♯ minor,
	Das wohltemperirte Clavier, i (1722)
BWV850	Prelude and fugue, D major,
	Das wohltemperirte Clavier, i (1722)
BWV851	Prelude and fugue, D minor,
	Das wohltemperirte Clavier, i (1722)
BWV852	Prelude and fugue, E♭ major,
	Das wohltemperirte Clavier, i (1722)
BWV853	Prelude and fugue, E♭ /D♯ minor,
	Das wohltemperirte Clavier, i (1722)
BWV854	Prelude and fugue, E major,
	Das wohltemperirte Clavier, i (1722)
BWV855	Prelude and fugue, E minor,
	Das wohltemperirte Clavier, i (1722)
BWV856	Prelude and fugue, F major,
	Das wohltemperirte Clavier, i (1722)
BWV857	Prelude and fugue, F minor,
	Das wohltemperirte Clavier, i (1722)
BWV858	Prelude and fugue, F♯ major,
	Das wohltemperirte Clavier, i (1722)
BWV859	Prelude and fugue, F♯ minor,
	Das wohltemperirte Clavier, i (1722)
BWV860	Prelude and fugue, G major,
	Das wohltemperirte Clavier, i (1722)

Prelude and fugue, G minor,	BWV861
Das wohltemperirte Clavier, i (1722)	
Prelude and fugue, A♭ major,	BWV862
Das wohltemperirte Clavier, i (1722)	
Prelude and fugue, G♯ minor,	BWV863
Das wohltemperirte Clavier, i (1722)	
Prelude and fugue, A major,	BWV864
Das wohltemperirte Clavier, i (1722)	
Prelude and fugue, A minor,	BWV865
Das wohltemperirte Clavier, i (1722)	
Prelude and fugue, B♭ major,	BWV866
Das wohltemperirte Clavier, i (1722)	
Prelude and fugue, B♭ minor,	BWV867
Das wohltemperirte Clavier, i (1722)	
Prelude and fugue, B major,	BWV868
Das wohltemperirte Clavier, i (1722)	
Prelude and fugue, B minor,	BWV869
Das wohltemperirte Clavier, i (1722)	
Prelude and fugue, C major,	BWV870
Das Wohltemperirte Clavier, ii (1738–42)	
Prelude and fugue, C minor,	BWV871
Das Wohltemperirte Clavier, ii (1738–42)	
Prelude and fugue, C♯ major,	BWV872
Das Wohltemperirte Clavier, ii (1738–42)	

BWV873	Prelude and fugue, C♯ minor, Das Wohltemperirte Clavier, ii (1738–42)
BWV874	Prelude and fugue, D major, Das Wohltemperirte Clavier, ii (1738–42)
BWV875	Prelude and fugue, D minor, Das Wohltemperirte Clavier, ii (1738–42)
BWV876	Prelude and fugue, E♭ major, Das Wohltemperirte Clavier, ii (1738–42)
BWV877	Prelude and fugue, E♭/D♯ minor, Das Wohltemperirte Clavier, ii (1738–42)
BWV878	Prelude and fugue, E major, Das Wohltemperirte Clavier, ii (1738–42)
BWV879	Prelude and fugue, E minor, Das Wohltemperirte Clavier, ii (1738–42)
BWV880	Prelude and fugue, F major, Das Wohltemperirte Clavier, ii (1738–42)
BWV881	Prelude and fugue, F minor, Das Wohltemperirte Clavier, ii (1738–42)
BWV882	Prelude and fugue, F♯ major, Das Wohltemperirte Clavier, ii (1738–42)
BWV883	Prelude and fugue, F♯ minor, Das Wohltemperirte Clavier, ii (1738–42)
BWV884	Prelude and fugue, G major, Das Wohltemperirte Clavier, ii (1738–42)

Prelude and fugue, G minor,	BWV885
Das Wohltemperirte Clavier, ii (1738–42)	
Prelude and fugue, A♭ major,	BWV886
Das Wohltemperirte Clavier, ii (1738–42)	
Prelude and fugue, G♯ minor,	BWV887
Das Wohltemperirte Clavier, ii (1738–42)	
Prelude and fugue, A major,	BWV888
Das Wohltemperirte Clavier, ii (1738–42)	
Prelude and fugue, A minor,	BWV889
Das Wohltemperirte Clavier, ii (1738–42)	
Prelude and fugue, B♭ major,	BWV890
Das Wohltemperirte Clavier, ii (1738–42)	
Prelude and fugue, B♭ minor,	BWV891
Das Wohltemperirte Clavier, ii (1738–42)	
Prelude and fugue, B major,	BWV892
Das Wohltemperirte Clavier, ii (1738–42)	
Prelude and fugue, B minor,	BWV893
Das Wohltemperirte Clavier, ii (1738–42)	
Prelude and fugue, keyboard, A minor (1708–17)	BWV894
Prelude and fugue, keyboard, A major (c. 1709)	BWV896
Prelude and fughetta, keyboard, E minor (c. 1720)	BWV900
Prelude and fughetta, keyboard, F major	BWV901
Prelude and fughetta, keyboard, G major	BWV902
Chromatic fantasia and fugue, keyboard, D minor (c. 1720)	BWV903

BWV904	Fantasia and fugue, keyboard, A minor (c. 1725)
BWV906	Fantasia and fugue, keyboard, C minor (c. 1738)
BWV910	Toccata, keyboard, F♯ minor (c. 1717)
BWV911	Toccata, keyboard, C minor (c. 1717)
BWV912	Toccata, keyboard, D major (c. 1710)
BWV913	Toccata, keyboard, D minor (before 1708)
BWV914	Toccata, keyboard, E minor (before 1708)
BWV915	Toccata, keyboard, G minor (before 1708)
BWV916	Toccata, keyboard, G major (c. 1719)
BWV924	Praeambulum, C major, Clavier-Büchlein for W. F. Bach (1720–)
BWV926	Prelude, D minor, Clavier-Büchlein for W. F. Bach (1720–)
BWV927	Praeambulum, F major, Clavier-Büchlein for W. F. Bach (1720–)
BWV928	Prelude, F major, Clavier-Büchlein for W. F. Bach (1720–)
BWV929	Trio, G minor, Clavier-Büchlein for W. F. Bach (1720–)
BWV930	Praeambulum, G minor, Clavier-Büchlein for W. F. Bach (1720–)
BWV933	Little prelude, C major, Clavierbüchlein for Anna Magdalena Bach (1722–5)
BWV934	Little prelude, C minor, Clavierbüchlein for Anna Magdalena Bach (1722–5)
BWV935	Little prelude, D minor, Clavierbüchlein for Anna Magdalena Bach (1722–5)
BWV936	Little prelude, D major, Clavierbüchlein for Anna Magdalena Bach (1722–5)

Little prelude, E major, Clavierbüchlein for Anna Magdalena Bach (1722–5)	BWV937
Little prelude, E minor, Clavierbüchlein for Anna Magdalena Bach (1722–5)	BWV938
Prelude, C major, Clavierbüchlein for Anna Magdalena Bach (1722–5)	BWV939
Prelude, D minor, Clavierbüchlein for Anna Magdalena Bach, (1722–5)	BWV940
Prelude, E minor, Clavierbüchlein for Anna Magdalena Bach, (1722–5)	BWV941
Prelude, A minor, Clavierbüchlein for Anna Magdalena Bach, (1722–5)	BWV942
Prelude, C major, Clavierbüchlein for Anna Magdalena Bach, (1722–5)	BWV943
Fugue, keyboard, A minor	BWV944
Fugue, keyboard, C major (c. 1708)	BWV946
Fugue on theme by Albinoni, keyboard, A major (c. 1710)	BWV950
Fugue on theme by Albinoni, keyboard, B minor (c. 1710)	BWV951
Fugue, C major, Clavier-Büchlein for W. F. Bach (1720–)	BWV953
Fugue, keyboard, B♭ major	BWV954
Fugue, keyboard, B♭ major	BWV955
Fugue, keyboard, A minor (c. 1710)	BWV958
Fugue, keyboard, A minor (c. 1710)	BWV959
Sonata, keyboard, D major (c. 1704)	BWV963

BWV965	Sonata, keyboard, A minor
BWV966	Sonata, keyboard, C major
BWV967	Sonata, keyboard, A minor
BWV971	Concerto nach italiänischen Gusto (Italian Concerto), Clavier-Übung, ii (1735)
BWV972	Concerto, keyboard, D major (1708–17)
BWV973	Concerto, keyboard, G major (1708–17)
BWV974	Concerto, keyboard, D minor (1708–17)
BWV975	Concerto, keyboard, G minor (1708–17)
BWV976	Concerto, keyboard, C major (1708–17)
BWV977	Concerto, keyboard, C major (1708–17)
BWV978	Concerto, keyboard, F major (1708–17)
BWV979	Concerto, keyboard, B minor (1708–17)
BWV980	Concerto, keyboard, G major (1708–17)
BWV981	Concerto, keyboard, C minor (1708–17)
BWV982	Concerto, keyboard, B♭ major (1708–17)
BWV983	Concerto, keyboard, G minor (1708–17)
BWV984	Concerto, keyboard, C major (1708–17)
BWV985	Concerto, keyboard, G minor (1708–17)
BWV986	Concerto, keyboard, G major (1708–17)
BWV987	Concerto, keyboard, D minor (1708–17)
BWV988	Aria mit verschiededenen Veraederungen (Goldberg Variations), Clavier-Übung, iv (1741–2)
BWV989	Aria variata, A minor, (before 1714)

Air with variations, C minor, Clavierbüchlein, i, for Anna Magdalena Bach (1722)	BWV991
Capriccio sopra la lontananza del suo fratellodilettissimo [Capriccio on the departure of his Most Beloved Brother], B♭ major (?1703, 1704 or 1706)	BWV992
Capriccio, keyboard, E major (c. 1704)	BWV993
Applicatio, C major, Clavier-Büchlein for W F Bach, (1720–)	BWV994
Suite, lute, G minor (1727–31)	BWV995
Suite, lute, E minor (c. 1708–17)	BWV996
Partita, lute, C minor (1737–41)	BWV997
Prelude, fugue and allegro, lute, E♭ major (1740s)	BWV998
Prelude, lute, C minor (c. 1720)	BWV999
Fugue, lute, G minor (c. 1725)	BWV1000
Sonata No. 1, solo violin, G minor (1720)	BWV1001
Partita No. 1, solo violin, B minor (1720)	BWV1002
Sonata No. 2, solo violin, A minor (1720)	BWV1003
Partita No. 2, solo violin, D minor (1720)	BWV1004
Sonata No. 3, solo violin, C major (1720)	BWV1005
Partita No. 3, solo violin, E major (1720)	BWV1006
Partita, lute, E major (1720)	BWV1006*a*
Suite, solo violin, G major (c. 1720)	BWV1007
Suite, solo violin, D minor (c. 1720)	BWV1008
Suite, solo violin, C major (c. 1720)	BWV1009
Suite, solo violin, E♭ major (c. 1720)	BWV1010

BWV1011	Suite, solo violin, C minor (c. 1720)
BWV1012	Suite, solo violin, D major (c. 1720)
BWV1013	Partita, flute, A minor (1720s)
BWV1014	Sonata No. 1, violin and harpsichord, B minor (1717–23)
BWV1015	Sonata No. 2, violin and harpsichord, A major (1717–23)
BWV1016	Sonata No. 3, violin and harpsichord, E major (1717–23)
BWV1017	Sonata No. 4, violin and harpsichord, C minor (1717–23)
BWV1018	Sonata No. 5, violin and harpsichord, F minor (1717–23)
BWV1019	Sonata No. 6, violin and harpsichord, G major (1717–23)
BWV1021	Sonata, violin and basso continuo, G major (before 1720)
BWV1023	Sonata, violin and basso continuo, E minor (1714–17)
BWV1027	Sonata, harpsichord and viola da gamba, G major (c. 1720)
BWV1027*a*	Trio, organ, G major
BWV1028	Sonata, harpsichord and viola da gamba, D major (c. 1720)
BWV1029	Sonata, harpsichord and viola da gamba, G minor (c. 1720)
BWV1030	Sonata, flute and harpsichord, B minor (1730s)
BWV1032	Sonata, flute and harpsichord, A major (1717–23)
BWV1034	Sonata, flute and basso continuo, E minor (1717–20)
BWV1035	Sonata, flute and basso continuo, E major (1717–20)
BWV1039	Trio sonata, G major (c. 1720)
BWV1040	Trio, F major (1713)
BWV1041	Violin concerto, A minor (1717–23)
BWV1042	Violin concerto, E major (1717–23)
BWV1043	Double violin concerto, D minor (1717–23)

Concerto, A minor (1730s)	BWV1044
Concerto movement for violin, D major	BWV1045
Brandenburg Concerto No. 1, F major (1717)	BWV1046
Sinfonia, F major (1713)	BWV1046*a*
Brandenburg Concerto No. 2, F major (1717–8)	BWV1047
Brandenburg Concerto No. 3, G major (1711–3)	BWV1048
Brandenburg Concerto No. 4, G major (c. 1720)	BWV1049
Brandenburg Concerto No. 5, D major (1720–1)	BWV1050
Brandenburg Concerto No. 6, B♭ major (1708–10)	BWV1051
Harpsichord concerto, D minor (1735–40)	BWV1052
Harpsichord concerto, E major (1735–40)	BWV1053
Harpsichord concerto, D major (1735–40)	BWV1054
Harpsichord concerto, A major (1735–40)	BWV1055
Harpsichord concerto, F minor (1735–40)	BWV1056
Harpsichord concerto, F major (1735–40)	BWV1057
Harpsichord concerto, G minor (1735–40)	BWV1058
Harpsichord concerto, D minor (1735–40)	BWV1059
Harpsichord concerto, C minor (1735–40)	BWV1060
Harpsichord concerto, C major (1735–40)	BWV1061
Harpsichord concerto, C minor (1735–40)	BWV1062
Harpsichord concerto, D minor (1735–40)	BWV1063
Harpsichord concerto, C major (1735–40)	BWV1064
Harpsichord concerto, A minor (1735–40)	BWV1065
Orchestral suite, C major (c. 1717–23)	BWV1066

BWV1067	Orchestral suite, B minor (1730s)
BWV1068	Orchestral suite, D major (1730s)
BWV1069	Orchestral suite, D major (c. 1717–23)
BWV1070	Overture, G minor
BWV1072	Canon trias harmonica (1713)
BWV1073	Canon a 4 perpetuus (1713)
BWV1074	Canon a 4 (1727)
BWV1075	Canon a 2 perpetuus (1734)
BWV1076	Canon triplex a 6
BWV1077	Canone doppio sopr'il soggetto (1747)
BWV1078	Canon super fa mi a 7 post tempus musicum (1749)
BWV1079	Musikalisches Opfer (1747)
BWV1080	Die Kunst der Fuge (c. 1745–50)
BWV1083	Credo (c. 1740)
BWV1086	Canon concordia discors
BWV1087	[14] Verschiedene Canones (1742–6)
A1–5	Fragments of church cantatas
A6–13, 18–9	Fragments of secular cantatas
A14–17, 20	Church cantatas, Lost

The most famous portrait of Bach, painted by Elias Gottlob Haussmann in 1746; he holds the score of his six-part Canon, BWV1076

j.s.bach

recommended recordings

These recordings are all available at the time of writing. The works are listed first, followed by details of the recording: the artists, record company and disc number. All numbers given are those that apply to the compact disc format but many recordings can also be bought on conventional tape cassette. Those suggested have been chosen from the many good ones available on the basis of personal response and experience, but need only be taken as a guide.

BWV1046–51	BRANDENBURG CONCERTOS NOS. 1–6
BWV 1066–9	ORCHESTRAL SUITES NOS. 1–4

ASMF, Marriner. EMI Dig. CDS7 47881-8 (3).
E. Concert, Pinnock. DG 423 492-2 (3).

BWV 1046–51	BRANDENBURG CONCERTOS NOS. 1–6

ASMF, Marriner. Philips 400 076/7-2 (2).

BWV1059/BWV35[1]	FLUTE CONCERTO IN E MINOR
BWV1067	SUITE NO. 2 IN B MINOR
BWV1039[2]	TRIO SONATA NO. 4 IN G MAJOR
BWV1079	THE MUSICAL OFFERING: TRIO SONATA IN C MINOR

Galway; [1]Zagreb Soloists, Ninic; [2] Chung, Moll, Welsh.
BMG/RCA GD 86517.

HARPSICHORD CONCERTOS

No. 1 in D minor	BWV1052
No. 2 in E major	BWV1053
No. 3 in D major	BWV1054
No. 4 in A major	BWV1055
No. 5 in F major	BWV1056
No. 6 in F major	BWV1057
No. 7 in G minor	BWV1058

Pinnock, E. Concert. DG Dig. 415 991-32 (Nos. 1-3); 415 992-2 (4- 7).

HARPSICHORD CONCERTOS

No. 2 in E major	BWV1053
No. 4 in A major	BWV1055
DOUBLE HARPSICHORD CONCERTO No. 2 in C major	BWV1061
TRIPLE HARPSICHORD CONCERTO No. 1 in D minor	BWV1063

Leppard, Davis, Ledger, ECO, Leppard. Philips 426 084-2.

HARPSICHORD CONCERTOS

No. 3 in D major	BWV1054
No. 6 in F major	BWV1057
No. 7 in G minor	BWV1058
DOUBLE HARPSICHORD CONCERTO No. 3 in C minor	BWV1062[1]

Leppard; [1]Ledger, ECO, Leppard. Philips 426 448-2.

CLAVIER CONCERTOS

BWV1052–8   NOS. 1–7

Schiff (pf), COE. Decca Dig. 425 676-2 (2).

CLAVIER CONCERTOS

BWV1052	NO. 1 IN D MINOR
BWV1053	NO. 2 IN E MAJOR
BWV1054	NO. 3 IN D MAJOR

Chang (pf), Cassovia, Stankovsky. Naxos Dig. 8.550422.

CLAVIER CONCERTOS

BWV1055	NO. 4 IN A MAJOR
BWV1056	NO. 5 IN F MINOR
BWV1057	NO. 6 IN F MINOR
BWV1058	NO. 7 IN G MINOR

Chang (pf), Cassovia, Stankovsky. Naxos Dig. 8.550423.

CLAVIER CONCERTOS

BWV1052	NO. 1 IN D MINOR
BWV1054	NO. 3 IN D MAJOR
BWV1056	NO. 5 IN F MINOR
BWV1057	NO. 6 IN F MINOR

Katsaris (pf), Liszt CO, Rolla. Teldec/Warner Dig. 9031 74779-2.

CLAVIER CONCERTOS

DOUBLE: NO. 1 IN C MINOR	BWV1060
DOUBLE: NO. 2 IN C	BWV1061
TRIPLE: IN D MINOR	BWV1063
QUADRUPLE: IN A MINOR	BWV1065

Eschenbach, Frantz, Oppitz, Schmidt, Hamburg PO, Eschenbach.
DG Dig. 415 655-2.

DOUBLE HARPSICHORD CONCERTOS NOS. 1 & 3	BWV1060/1062
DOUBLE CONCERTO FOR VIOLIN AND OBOE IN C MINOR	BWV1060
DOUBLE VIOLIN CONCERTO IN D MINOR	BWV1043

Schröder, Hirons, Rousset, Hogwood, Mackintosh, Hammer, AAM,
Hogwood. O-L Dig. 421 500-2.

OBOE CONCERTOS

IN A MAJOR	BWV1055
IN D MINOR	BWV1059
IN F MAJOR	BWV1053

Holliger, ASMF, Brown. Philips Dig. 415 851-2.

ORGAN CONCERTOS

BWV146/1052	No. 1 IN D MINOR
BWV49/169/1053	No. 2 IN D MAJOR
BWV35/1059	No. 3 IN D MINOR
BWV1045	SINFONIA IN D MAJOR
BWV29	CANTATA
	SINFONIA

(Reconstructed and ed. Schurck) Hurford, N. Sinfonia, Hickox. Argo Dig. 425 479-2; 425 479-4.

VIOLIN CONCERTOS

BWV1041[1]	No. 1 IN A MINOR
BWV1042[2]	No. 2 IN E MAJOR
BWV1043[3]	DOUBLE VIOLIN CONCERTO IN D MINOR
BWV1060[4]	DOUBLE CONCERTO FOR VIOLIN & OBOE IN D MINOR

Grumiaux;[3] Krebbers, [4]Holliger; [1-3]Les Solistes Romandes, Gerecz; [4]New Philh. O, de Waart. Philips 420 700-2. Kremer; [4]Holliger; ASMF. Philips Dig. 432 0036-2.

VIOLIN CONCERTOS

NO. 1 IN A MINOR	BWV1041
NO. 2 IN E MAJOR	BWV1042
DOUBLE VIOLIN concerto IN D MINOR	BWV1043[1]
VIOLIN AND OBOE CONCERTO IN C MINOR	BWV1060[2]

[1]Garcia (vn); [2]Black (ob); ECO, Sitkovetsky (vn). Novalis 150 017-2.

THE MUSICAL OFFERING	BWV1079

ASMF, Marriner. Philips 412 800-2.

ORCHESTRAL SUITES

NO. 1 IN C MAJOR	BWV1066
NO. 2 IN B MINOR	BWV1067
NO. 3 IN D MAJOR	BWV1068
NO. 4 IN D MAJOR	BWV1069

ASMF, Marriner. Decca 430 378-2; 430 378-4.
AAM, Hogwood. O-L Dig. 417 834-2.

ORCHESTRAL SUITES NOS. 1–4	BWV1066–9
THE MUSICAL OFFERING	BWV1079

Bath Festival O. (members), Menuhin.
EMI CZS 767350-2 (2); for Suites only:
EG 764266-4.

BWV812–7	**FRENCH SUITES**
	Leonhardt (hpd). RCA Victor Seon GD 71963.
	From Philips 6709 500.

CELLO SUITES

BWV1007	NO. 1 IN G MAJOR
BWV1008	NO. 2 IN D MINOR
BWV1009	NO. 3 IN C MAJOR
BWV1010	NO. 4 IN E♭ MAJOR
BWV1011	NO. 5 IN C MINOR
BWV1012	NO. 6 IN D MINOR

Schiff. EMI Dig. CDS7 47471-8 (2).

Gendron. Philips 422 494-2; 422 494-4

(Nos. 1, 4 & 6); 422 495-2; 422 495-4 (Nos. 2, 3 & 5).

Ma. Sony Dig. M2K 37867 (2).

FLUTE SONATAS

BWV1030–5	NOS. 1–6
BWV1020	IN G MINOR
BWV1013	PARTITA IN A MINOR

Larrieu, Puyana, Kuijken. Philips 422 943-2 (2).

LUTE SUITES (ARR. FOR GUITAR)

NO. 1 IN G MINOR	BWV995
NO. 2 IN E MINOR	BWV996
PARTITA IN C MINOR	BWV997
PARTITA IN E MAJOR	BWV1006A

Williams (guitar). Sony MK 42204.

LUTE SUITES (ARR. FOR GUITAR)

NOS. 1–2	BWV996–7
FUGUE IN G MINOR	BWV1000

Söllscher (guitar). DG Dig. 410643-2.

TRIO SONATAS (ARR. FOR GUITAR)

NO. 1 IN D MINOR	BWV1036
NO. 2 IN C MAJOR	BWV1037
NOS. 3 & 4 IN G MINOR	BWV 1038–9

London Baroque. HM Dig. HMC 901173, HMC 401173.

VIOLA DA GAMBA SONATAS

NOS. 1–3	BWV1027–9

Ma (vc), Cooper. Sony Dig. MK 37794.
Kuijken, Leonhardt. HM/BMG GD 77044.

BWV1001, 1003, 1005	Violin Sonatas Nos. 1–3
BWV1002, 1004, 1006	Violin partitas Nos. 1–3

Sitkovetsky. Orfeo C 130853H (2).

Perlman. EMI Dig. CDS7 49483-2 (2).

BWV1006	Partita in E major
BWV1013	Sonata in A minor (trans. G minor)
BWV1003	Sonata in A minor

(arr. Bylsma). Bylsma (vc piccolo). DHM RD77998.

TRS. WORKS FOR UNACCOMPANIED VIOLIN

BWV1001	Sonata in G minor
BWV1005	Sonata in D major
BWV1012	Suite in D major (from Suite for viola pomposa)

Leonhardt (hpd). HM/BMG GD 77014 [77014-2-RG].

VIOLIN SONATAS (FOR VIOLIN AND HARPSICHORD)

BWV1014–9	Nos. 1–6

Kuijken, Leonhardt. HM/BMG GD 77170 (2).

SONATAS AND PARTITAS FOR SOLO VIOLIN

BWV1001	Sonata No. 1 in G minor
BWV1003	Sonata No. 2 in A minor
BWV1005	Sonata No. 3 in C major

Partita No.1 in B minor	BWV1002
Partita No. 2 in D minor	BWV1004
Partita No. 3 in E major	BWV1006

Szeryng (vn). CBS Masterworks Portrait mono CD46721.

The Art of Fugue	BWV1080

DG Dig. 427 673-2. Gilbert (hpd).

The Art of Fugue	BWV1080
Italian concerto	BWV971
Partita in B minor	BWV831
Prelude, fugue and allegro in E♭ major	BWV998

Leonhardt (hpd). HM/BMG GD 77013 (2).

Capriccio in B♭ major	BWV992
Fantasia and fugue in A minor	BWV904
Prelude, fugue and allegro in E♭ major	BWV998
Suite in E minor	BWV996
Toccata in E minor	BWV914

Leonhardt (hpd). Philips Dig. 416 141-2.

Chromatic fantasia and fugue in D minor	BWV903
Fantasia in C minor	BWV906
Fantasia in G minor	BWV917

BWV919	FANTASIA IN C MINOR
BWV904	FANTASIA AND FUGUE IN A MINOR
BWV921	PRELUDE IN C MINOR
BWV922	PRELUDE IN A MINOR
BWV894	PRELUDE AND FUGUE IN A MINOR
BWV901	PRELUDE AND FUGUE IN F MAJOR
BWV902	PRELUDE AND FUGUE IN G MAJOR
	Staier (hpd). HM/BMG RD 77039.

BWV903	CHROMATIC FANTASIA AND FUGUE IN D MINOR
BWV971	ITALIAN CONCERTO
BWV825	PARTITA NO. 1 IN B♭ MAJOR
BWV998	PRELUDE, FUGUE AND ALLEGRO IN E♭ MAJOR
BWV916	TOCCATA, ADAGIO AND FUGUE IN G MAJOR
	Cole. Virgin Dig. VC7 90712-2; VC7 90712-4.

TOCCATAS

BWV910	F♯ MINOR
BWV911	C MINOR
BWV912	D MAJOR
BWV913	D MINOR
BWV914	E MINOR
BWV915	G MINOR
BWV916	G MAJOR
	van Asperen (hpd). EMI Reflexe CDC7 54081-2.

PRELUDE AND FUGUE IN C MAJOR	BWV531
PRELUDE AND FUGUE IN G MINOR	BWV535
PRELUDE AND FUGUE IN D MINOR	BWV539
CONCERTO No. 1 IN G MAJOR	BWV592
FANTASIA IN G MAJOR	BWV572
PRELUDE IN C MAJOR	BWV567
'LITTLE' FUGUE IN G MINOR	BWV578
CANZONA IN D MINOR	BWV588
CHORALE PRELUDE 'IN DULCI JUBILO'	BWV751

Murray (org). Telarc CD80179.

4 DUETS	BWV 802–5
ENGLISH SUITE No. 6 IN D MINOR	BWV811
ITALIAN CONCERTO	BWV971
TOCCATA IN C MINOR	BWV911

Hewitt (pf). DG Dig. 429 975-2; 429 975-4.

ENGLISH SUITES

Nos. 1–6	BWV806–11

Schiff (pf). Decca Dig. 421 640-2 (2).

FRENCH SUITES Nos. 1–6	BWV812–7
CAPRICCIO	BWV992

Dreyfus (hpd). DG 427 149-2 (2).

BWV988	**GOLDBERG VARIATIONS** van Asperen (hpd). EMI Dig. CDC7 54209-2. Dreyfus (hpd). Denon Dig. CO 73677.

| BWV988
BWV968
BWV903
BWV906/1
BWV 902/1 | **GOLDBERG VARIATIONS**
ADAGIO IN G MAJOR
CHROMATIC FANTASIA AND FUGUE IN D MINOR
FANTASIA IN C MINOR
PRELUDE IN G MAJOR
Black (hpd). Collins 7003-2 (2). |

| BWV 772–86
BWV 787–801 | **15 2–PART INVENTIONS**
15 3–PART INVENTIONS
Gilbert (hpd). DG Dig. 415 112-2.
Dreyfus (hpd). Denon Dig. C37 7566. |

| BWV 825–30 | **PARTITAS NOS. 1-6**
Schiff (pf). Decca Dig. 411 732-2 (2). |

| BWV846–93 | **THE WELL-TEMPERED CLAVIER (BOOKS 1 AND 2)**
Gilbert (hpd). DG Dig. 413 439-2 (4). |

ORGAN PARTITAS

CHRIST, DER DU BIST DER HELLE TAG	BWV766
O GOTT, DU FROMMER GOTT	BWV767
SEI GEGRÜSSET, JESU GÜTIG	BWV768
ACH, WAS SOLL ICH SÜNDER MACHEN?	BWV770

Preston. DG 429 775-2GH.

TOCCATA AND FUGUE IN D MINOR	BWV565
TOCCATA AND FUGUE IN F MAJOR	BWV540
TOCCATA AND FUGUE IN D MINOR, 'DORIAN'	BWV538
TOCCATA, ADAGIO AND FUGUE IN C MAJOR	BWV564
PASSACAGLIA AND FUGUE IN C MINOR	BWV582

Herrick. Hyperion CDA66434.

TOCCATA AND FUGUE IN D MINOR, 'DORIAN'	BWV538
PARTITA ON 'SEI GEGRÜSSET, JESU GUTIG'	BWV768
FANTASIA IN G MAJOR	BWV572
TRIO SONATA NO. 6 IN G MAJOR	BWV530
CHORALE PRELUDE, 'VATER UNSER IM HIMMELREICH'	BWV682
CHORALE PRELUDE, JESU CHRISTUS UNSER HEILAND	BWV688
PRELUDE AND FUGUE IN A MINOR	BWV543

Volume 3. Koopman (org). Novalis 150036-2.

BWV645	CHORALE PRELUDE: WACHET AUF, RUFT UNS DIE STIMME
BWV659	CHORALE PRELUDE: NUN KOMM' DER HEIDEN HEILAND
BWV678	CHORALE PRELUDE: DIES SIND DIE HEIL' GEN ZEHN GEBOT'
BWV706	CHORALE PRELUDE: LIEBSTER JESU, WIR SIND HIER
BWV709	CHORALE PRELUDE: HERR JESU CHRIST, DICH ZU UNS WEND'
BWV721	CHORALE PRELUDE: ERBARM' DICH MEIN, O HERRE GOTT
BWV727	CHORALE PRELUDE: HERZLICH THUT MICH VERLANGEN
BWV737	CHORALE PRELUDE: VATER UNSER IM HIMMELREICH
BWV745	CHORALE PRELUDE: AUS DER TIEFE RUFE ICH
BWV572	FANTASIA IN G MAJOR
BWV543	PRELUDE AND FUGUE IN A MINOR
BWV546	PRELUDE AND FUGUE IN C MINOR
BWV565	TOCCATA AND FUGUE IN D MINOR
	Danby (org). CBS Dig. CD45807.

| BWV599–644 | ORGELBÜCHLEIN |
| | Preston (org.) DG 431 816-2GH. |

BWV565	ADAGIO IN C
BWV727	CHORALE: HERZLICH TUT MICH VERLANGEN
BWV730	CHORALE: LIEBSTER JESU
BWV645	CHORALE: WACHET AUF
BWV542	FANTASIA AND FUGUE IN G MINOR
BWV552	FUGUE IN E♭ MAJOR, 'ST. ANNE'

Passacaglia and fugue in C minor	BWV582
Toccata and fugue in D minor	BWV565

Hurford (org). Decca 417 711-2.

Allabreve in D major	BWV589
Chorale prelude: Ach Gott und Herr	BWV714
Preludes and fugues	BWV532/553–560
Toccata and fugue in D minor	BWV565

Sanger (org). Mer. ECD 84081.

35 Arnstadt chorale preludes	BWV714/719/957/742/
	1090–1120
Chorale prelude: Ich Ruf' zu dir	BWV639
Prelude and fugue in C major	BWV531
Prelude and fugue in D minor	BWV549*a*
Prelude and fugue in G minor	BWV535
Prelude and fugue in E major	BWV566

Barber (org).ASV Gaudeamus Dig. CD GAU 120.121; ZC GAU 120/121
(available separately).

Chorale prelude: Ich ruf' zu dir, Herr Jesu Christ	BWV639
Chorale prelude: Nun Komm der Heiden Heiland	BWV659
Schübler chorale: Wachet auf	BWV645
Fantasia and fugue in G minor	BWV542

BWV767	Partita: O Gott, du frommer Gott
BWV552	Prelude and fugue in E♭ major, 'St. Anne'
BWV565	Toccata and fugue in D minor
	Koopman (org). Novalis Dig. 150 005-2.

BWV682	Chorale prelude: Vater unser in Himmelreich
BWV688	Chorale prelude: Jesu Christus, unser Heiland
BWV572	Fantasia in G major
BWV768	Partita: Sei gegrüsset, Jesu gütig
BWV543	Prelude and fugue in A minor
BWV538	Toccata and fugue in D minor, 'Dorian'
BWV530	Trio sonata in G major
	Koopman (org). Novalis Dig. 150 036-2.

BWV572	Fantasia in G major
BWV545	Prelude and fugue in C major
BWV549–50	Preludes and fugues in G major
BWV535	Prelude and fugue in G minor
BWV590	Pastorale in F major
BWV565	Toccata and fugue in D minor
	Rübsam (org). Philips 420 860-2.

| BWV542 | Fantasia and fugue in G minor |
| BWV590 | Pastorale in F major |

Passacaglia and Fugue in C minor	BWV582
Prelude and Fugue in A minor	BWV543
Prelude and Fugue in B minor	BWV544
Prelude and Fugue in C major	BWV545

Power Biggs (org). Sony SBK 46551.

8 Little Preludes and Fugues	BWV553–60
Prelude and Fugue in D major	BWV532
Toccata, Adagio and Fugue in C major	BWV564
Trio Sonata No. 1 in E♭ major	BWV525

Koopman (org). ASV Novalis Dig. 150 066-2; 150 066-4.

6 Schübler Chorales	BWV645–50
Pastorale in F major	BWV590
Passacaglia in C minor	BWV582
Toccata, Adagio and Fugue in C major	BVWV564
Toccata and Fugue in D minor	BWV565

Koopman (org). DG Dig. 427 801-2; 427 801-4.

CANTATAS

Nun danket alle Gott	BWV192[1]
Höchsterwünschtes Freudenfest	BWV194[2]
Dem Gerechten muss das Licht immer wieder aufgehen	BWV195[3]

BWV196[4]	DER HERR DENKET AN UNS
BWV197[5]	GOTT IST UNSER ZUVERSICHT
BWV198[6]	LASS, FÜSTIN, LASS NOCH EINEN STRAHL
BWV199[7]	MEIN HERZE SCHWIMMT IM BLUT

[1,4]Wittek, [1]Stricker, [2]Gienger, [3,5,6]O Farrell, [7]Bonney, [3,5,6]Jacabs, [3,6]Elwes, [2,4]Equilvz,[1,2,4]Hampson, [3,5,6]van der Kamp, [1,2,4]Tölz Boys' Choir, Hanover Boy's Choir; [3,5,6]Ghent Collegium Vocale; [1,2,4,6]Vienna Concentus Musicus, Harnoncourt; [3,5,6]Leonhardt Consort, Leonhardt.

Volumes 44 and 45. Teldec Das Alte Werk 244 193/4-2.

SECULAR CANTATAS

BWV202	WEICHET NUR, BETRÜBTE SCHATTEN,'WEDDING CANTATA'
BWV209[1]	NON SA CHE SIA DOLORE
BWV211[1,2,3]	SCHWEIGT STILLE, PLAUDERT NICHT, 'COFFEE CANTATA'
BWV212[1,2,3]	MER HAHN EN NEUE OBERKEET, 'PEASANT CANTATA'

[1]Ameling (sop); [2]English (ten); [3]Nimsgern (bass); Collegium Aureum. DHM GD77151. From BASF BAC3052/3 (9/74).

BWV10	CANTATA: MEINE SEELE ERHEBT DEN HERRN
BWV249	EASTER ORATORIO

Ameling, Watts, Krenn, Rintzler, Vienna Academy Ch., Stuttgart CO, Münchinger. Decca 425 650-2.

CANTATA: JAUCHZET GOTT IN ALLEN LANDEN   BWV51
MAGNIFICAT IN D MAJOR   BWV243

Kirkby, E. Bar. Soloists, Gardiner. Philips Dig. 411 458-2.

CANTATAS

WIDERSTEHE DOCH DER SÜNDE   BWV54
GOT SOL ALLEIN   BWV169
VERGNÜGTE RUH'   BWV170

Bowman, King's Consort, King. Hyp. Dig. CDA 66326; KA 66326.

CANTATAS

ICH WILL DEN KREUZSTAB GERNE TRAGEN   BWV56
ICH HABE GENUG   BWV82[1]
DER FRIEDE SEI MIT DIR   BWV158

Opalach, [1]Monahan, Stevens, Hite; Bach Ens., Rifkin. O-L Dig. 425 822-2.

CANTATAS

SELIG IST DER MANN   BWV57
ACH GOTT, WIE MANCHES   BWV58
WER MICH LIEBER   BWV59
TRITT AUF DIE GLAUBENSBAHN   BWV152

Zádori, Polgár, Savaria Vocal Ens.,
Capella Savaria, Pál Németh. Hung. Dig. HCD 12897.

CANTATAS

BWV67	HALT IM GEDÄCHTNIS JESUM CHRIST
BWV130	HERR GOTT, DICH LOBEN ALLE WIR
BWV243	MAGNIFICAT IN D MAJOR

Ameling, Watts, Krenn, Krause, Lausanne Pro Arte Ch., SRO, Ansermet. Decca 433 175-2.

CANTATAS

BWV80	EIN FESTE BURG IST UNSER GOTT
BWV140	WACHET AUF, RUFT UNS DIE STIMME

Fontana, Hamari, Winbergh, Krause, Humnus Boys' Ch., SCO, Münchinger. Decca Dig. 414 045-2.

CANTATAS

BWV82[1,2]	ICH HABE GENUG
BWV159[1,3,4]	SEHET, WIR GEHN HINAUF GEN JERUSALEM
BWV170[3]	VERGNÜGTE RUH', ELIEBTE SEELENLUST

[1]Shirley-Quirk; [2]Lord; [3]Baker; [4]Tear, St. Anthony Singers; ASMF, Marriner. Decca 430 260-2; 430 260-4.

CANTATAS

Gottes Zeit ist die allerbeste Zeit	BWV106
O Jesu Christ, mein Lebens Licht	BWV118
Lass, Fürstin, lass noch einen Strahl	BWV198

Argenta, Chance, Rolfe Johnson, Varcoe, Monteverdi Ch., E. Bar. Soloists,
Gardiner. DG Dig 429 782-2.

CANTATAS

Gottes Zeit ist die allerbeste Zeit	BWV106
Aus der Tiefen	BWV131

Monoyios, Rickards, Brownlees, Opalach, Bach Ens., Rifkin.
O-L Dig. 417 323-2

CANTATA

Der zufriedengestellte Äolus	BWV205

Kenny, Lipovšek, Equiluz, Holl, Arnold-Schönberg Ch., VCM,
Harnoncourt. Teledec/Warner Dig. 2292 42957-2.

CANTATAS

Schleicht, spielende Wellen	BWV206
Auf, schmetternde Töne der muntern Trompeten	BWV207*a*

Ziesak, Chance, Prégardien, Kooy, Stuttgart Chamber Ch., Cologne
Concerto/Bernius. Sony Classical Vivarte CD46492.

CANTATA

BWV208   WAS MIR BEHAGT, IST NUR DIE MUNTRE JAGD (HUNT CANTATA)
Smith, Kirby, Davis, George, Parley of Instruments, Goodman. Hyp. Dig.
CDA 66169; KA 66169.

CANTATAS

BWV211   SCHWEIGT STILLE, PLAUDERT NICHT 'COFFEE' CANTATA
BWV212   MER HAHN EN NEUE OBERKEET 'PEASANT' CANTATA
Kirkby, Rogers, Covey-Crump, Thomas, AAM, Hogwood.
O-L Dig. 417 621-2.

BWV248   CHRISTMAS ORATORIO
Donath, Ihle, Lipovsek, Schreier, Buchner, Holl, Leipzig R.Ch., Dresden
State O, Schreier. Philips Dig. 420 204-2 (3).

BWV248   CHRISTMAS ORATORIO
BWV243   MAGNIFICAT IN D MAJOR
Ameling, Watts, Pears, Krause, Ch., Stuttgart CO, Münchinger.
Decca 425 441-2 (3).

Magnificat in D major   BWV243
Cantata: Jauchzet Gott in allen Landen!   BWV51

Argenta, Kwella, Kirkby, Brett, Rolfe Johnson, David Thomas, E. Bar.
Soloists, Gardiner. Ph Dig. 411 458-2.

Mass in B minor   BWV232

Argenta, Dawson, Fairfield, Knibbs, Kwella, Hall, Nichols, Chance, Collin,
Stafford, Evans, Milner, Murgatroyd, Lloyd-Morgan, Varcoe, Monteverdi
Ch., E. Bar. Soloists, Gardiner. DG Dig. 415 514-2.
Kirkby, Van Evera, Iconomou, Immler, Kilian, Covey-Crump, Thomas,
Taverner Consort, Taverner Players/Parrott. EMI CDS7 47293-8.

MASSES
in F major   BWV233[1]
in A major   BWV234
in G minor   BWV235[2]
in G major   BWV236

[1]Giebel, Litz, Prey, Lausanne Pro Arte Ch., Munich Pro Arte O, Redel;
[2]Ameling, Finnilä, Altmeyer, Reimer, Westphalian Singers, German Bach
Soloists, Winschermann. Philips. 432 494-2 (2).

MOTETS
Singet dem Herrn ein Neues Lied   BWV225
Der Geist hilft unser Schwachheit   BWV226

BWV227   JESU MEINE FREUDE
BWV228   DER GERECHTE KOMMT UM FÜRCHTE DICH NICHT
BWV229   KOMM, JESU, KOMM
BWV230   LOBET DEN HERRN
BWV231   SEI LOB UND PREIS MIT EHREN

Regensburger Domspätzen, Hamburg Bläswerkreis, V. Capella Academica,
Schneidt. DG 435 087-2; 435 087-4.

BWV245   ST. JOHN PASSION

Rolfe Johnson, Varcoe, Hauptmann, Argenta & soloists, Monteverdi Ch., E.
Bar. Sol., Gardiner. DG Dig. 419 324-2 (2).

BWV244   ST. MATTHEW PASSION

Schreier, Adam, Popp, Lipovsek, Holl, Dresden Childrens' Ch., Leipzig R.
Ch., Dresden State O, Schreier. Ph. Dig. 412 527-2 (3).
Pears, Fischer-Dieskau, Schwarzkopf, Ludwig, Gedda, Berry, Hampstead
Parish Church Ch., Philh. Ch. & O, Klemperer. EMI CMS7 63058-2 (3).

BWV244   ST. MATTHEW PASSION: ARIAS AND CHORUSES

Bonney, Monoyois, Von Otter, Chance, Crook, Hauptmann, Monteverdi Ch.,
L. Oratory Junior Ch., E. Bar. Soloists, Gardiner.
DG Dig. 435 089-2; 435 089-4.

ARIAS

BIST DU BEI MIR	BWV508
CANTATA: WEICHET NUR, BETRUBTE SCHATTEN	BWV202
CANTATA: RICETTI GRAMEZZA	BWV209
ST. MATTHEW PASSION: BLUTE NUR; ICH WILL DIR MEIN HERZE SCHENKEN	BWV244

Augér, Mostly Mozart O, Schwartz. Delos Dig. D/CD 3026

AAM *Academy of Ancient Music*
arr. *arranged/arrangement*
ASMF *Academy of St. Martin-in-the-Fields*
attrib. *attributed*
bar. *baritone*
bc. *basso continuo*
bn. *bassoon*
c. *circa*
ch. *chorus/choir/chorale*
Chan. *Chandos*
cl. *clarinet*
CO *Chamber Orchestra*
COE *Chamber Orchestra of Europe*
comp. *composed/composition*
contr. *contralto*
db. *double bass*
DG *Deutsche Grammophon*
Dig. *digital recording*
dir. *director*
ECO *English Chamber Orchestra*
ed. *editor/edited*
edn. *edition*
ens. *ensemble*
fl. *flute*
HM *Harmonia Mundi France*
hn. *horn*
hp. *harp*
hpd. *harpsichord*
Hung. *Hungaroton*

instr. *instrument/instrumental*
kbd. *keyboard*
LSO *London Symphony Orchestra*
Mer. *Meridian*
mez. *mezzo-soprano*
ob. *oboe*
OCO *Orpheus Chamber Orchestra*
orch. *orchestra/orchestral/orchestrated*
org. *organ/organist*
O-L *Oiseau-Lyre*
perc. *percussion*
pf. *pianoforte*
picc. *piccolo*
PO *Philharmonic Orchestra*
qnt. *quintet*
qt. *quartet*
sop. *soprano*
str. *string(s)*
tb. *trombone*
ten. *tenor*
tpt. *trumpet*
trans. *translated/translation*
transcr. *transcribed/transcription*
unacc. *unaccompanied*
va. *viola*
var. *various/variation*
vc. *cello*
vn. *violin*

- SELECTED FURTHER READING -

F Blume, *Two Centuries of Bach* (Kassel, 1947; English trans. 1950)

Jan Chiapusso, *Bach's World* (Indiana University Press, 1968)

H T David & A Mendel, *The Bach Reader* (New York, 1945)

A E F Dickinson, *The Art of J. S. Bach* (London, 1935, rev. edn. 1950)

Imogen Holst, *Bach* (Faber, 1965)

Malcolm Macdonald, *Bach* (Dent 'Master Musicians', 1982)

C H Parry, *Johann Sebastian Bach* (Putnam, 1909)

C S Terry, *Bach: A Biography* (London, 1928)

C S Terry, *The Music of Bach* (London, 1933)

Hannsdieter Wohlfarth, *Johann Sebastian Bach* (Fortress Press, Philadelphia 1985)

Percy M Young, *The Bachs, 1500–1850* (London, 1970)

- ACKNOWLEDGEMENTS -

The publishers wish to thank the following copyright holders
for their permission to reproduce illustrations supplied:

Archiv Für Kunst und Geschichte, Berlin
The Bridgeman Art Library
The Mansell Collection Ltd

1–3. **Brandenburg concerto, No.3, BWV1048**   11'33"
I Musici
With its two busy movements separated by a brief cadence of slower music, the Third Brandenburg Concerto provides a famous example of Bach's musical vigour and good humour.

4–5. **The Well–Tempered Klavier Book 1, Prelude & Fugue No. 1 in C, BWV846**   5'18"
Friedrich Gulda
The flowing First Prelude in Book 1 of the 'Forty-Eight' almost dispenses with melody as such, and the French composer Gounod added one to it to create one of the most famous of sacred songs.

6. **Air on a G String, from Suite No. 3, BWV808**   5'33"
English Chamber Orchestra/Raymond Leppard
Bach's own melodic style is seen at its finest in this great string melody.

7. **Toccata & Fugue in D minor, BWV565**   11'34"
Daniel Chorzempa
Great cathedrals of sound rise, fall and are rebuilt in this dazzling organ work of Bach's early maturity.

8. Mass in B minor, Gloria: Cum Sancto Spirito, BWV232   4'18"
RIAS Chamber Chior, Leipzig Radio Symphony Orchestra/Lorin Maazel
This excerpt from the B minor Mass glorifies God in buoyant, bustling music.

9. Concerto for 2 violins, 2nd movement, BWV1043   6'40"
Arthur Grumiaux, Herman Krebbers, Philharmonia Orchestra/Edo de Waart
*Another example of Bach's lyrical melodic vein, in which the two solo
violins' interplay of lines resembles the graceful flight of two birds at sunset.*

10. 'Peasant' Cantata,
'Klein – Zschocher müsse so zart und süsse', BWV212   6'06"
Julia Varady, Academy of St. Martin-in-the-Fields/Sir Neville Marriner
*The mood of this quasi-operatic aria is bucolic, befitting a text written in homespun local
German dialect for performance at the estate near Leipzig, named Kleinzschocher, of the
country landowner Carl Heinrich von Dieskau.*

11. Chaconne for solo violin in D minor, BWV1004   13'17"
Arthur Grumiaux
*Built on a sequence of harmonies heard at the start and then repeated with
variations, this music for solo violin shows Bach's profound understanding
of this instrument which he himself played with skill.*

12. St. Matthew Passion, final chorus, BWV244   6'59"
   Agnes Giebel, Marga Höffgen, Ernst Haefliger, Karl Ridderbusch,
   Netherlands Radio Chorus/Royal Concertgebouw Orchestra/Eugen Jochum
   A sublime sarabande, 'In Tears of Grief' is the final chorus at the ending
   of the Passion story as Bach and his librettist Picander told it to their
   Leipzig congregation on Good Friday, April 11, 1727.